Cont

The Hope of Salvation for Infants who die without being Baptised*

The International Theological Commission has studied the question of the fate of un-baptised infants, bearing in mind the principle of the "hierarchy of truths" and the other theological principles of the universal salvific will of God, the unicity and insuperability of the mediation of Christ, the sacramentality of the Church in the order of salvation, and the reality of Original Sin. In the contemporary context of cultural relativism and religious pluralism the number of non-baptized infants has grown considerably, and therefore the reflection on the possibility of salvation for these infants has become urgent. The Church is conscious that this salvation is attainable only in Christ through the Spirit. But the Church, as mother and teacher, cannot fail to reflect upon the fate of all men, created in the image of God, and in a more particular way on the fate of the weakest members of the human family and those who are not yet able to use their reason and freedom.

---

* PRELIMINARY NOTE: The theme "The Hope of Salvation for Infants who Die Without Being Baptized" was placed under the study of the International Theological Commission. In order to prepare for this study, a Committee was formed comprised by Most Rev. Ignazio Sanna, Most Rev. Basil Kyu-Man Cho, Rev. Peter Damien Akpunonu, Rev. Adelbert Denaux, Rev. Gilles Emery, OP, Msgr. Ricardo Ferrara, Msgr. István Ivancsó, Msgr. Paul McPartlan, Rev. Dominic Veliath, SDB (President of the Committee), and Sr. Sarah Butler, MSTB. The Committee also received the collaboration of Rev. Luis Ladaria, SJ, the Secretary General of the International Theological Commission, and Msgr. Guido Pozzo, the Assistant to the ITC, as well as other members of the Commission. The general discussion on the theme took place during the plenary sessions of the ITC, held in Rome. In October 2005 and October 2006. This present text was approved *in forma specifica* by the members of the Commission, and was subsequently submitted to its President, Cardinal William Levada who, upon receiving the approval of the Holy father in an audience granted on 19th January, 2007, approved the text for publication.

It is clear that the traditional teaching on this topic has concentrated on the theory of *limbo*, understood as a state which includes the souls of infants who die subject to original sin and without baptism, and who, therefore, neither merit the beatific vision, nor yet are subjected to any punishment, because they are not guilty of any personal sin. This theory, elaborated by theologians beginning in the Middle Ages, never entered into the dogmatic definitions of the Magisterium, even if that same Magisterium did at times mention the theory in its ordinary teaching up until the Second Vatican Council. It remains therefore a possible theological hypothesis. However, in the *Catechism of the Catholic Church* (1992), the theory of limbo is not mentioned. Rather, the Catechism teaches that infants who die without baptism are entrusted by the Church to the mercy of God, as is shown in the specific funeral rite for such children. The principle that God desires the salvation of all people gives rise to the hope that there is a path to salvation for infants who die without baptism (cf. *CCC*, 1261), and therefore also to the theological desire to find a coherent and logical connection between the diverse affirmations of the Catholic faith: the universal salvific will of God; the unicity of the mediation of Christ; the necessity of baptism for salvation; the universal action of grace in relation to the sacraments; the link between original sin and the deprivation of the beatific vision; the creation of man "in Christ".

The conclusion of this study is that there are theological and liturgical reasons to hope that infants who die without baptism may be saved and brought into eternal happiness, even if there is not an explicit teaching on this question found in Revelation. However, none of the considerations proposed in this text to motivate a new approach to the question may be used to negate the necessity of baptism, nor to delay the conferral of the sacrament. Rather, there are reasons to hope that God will save these infants precisely because it was not possible to do for them that what would have been most desirable - to baptize them in the faith of the Church and incorporate them visibly into the Body of Christ.

Finally, an observation on the methodology of the text is necessary. The treatment of this theme must be placed within the historical development of the faith. According to *Dei Verbum* 8, the factors that contribute to this development are the reflection and the study of the faithful, the experience of spiritual things, and the teaching of the Magisterium. When the question of infants who die without baptism was first taken up in the history of Christian thought, it is possible that the doctrinal nature of the question or its implications were not fully understood. Only when seen in light of the historical development of theology over the course of time until Vatican II does this specific question find its proper context within Catholic doctrine. Only in this way - and observing the principle of the hierarchy of truths mentioned in the Decree of the Second Vatican Council *Unitatis redintegratio* (#11) – the topic can be reconsidered explicitly under the global horizon of the faith of the Church. This Document, from the point of view of speculative theology as well as from the practical and pastoral perspective, constitutes for a useful and timely mean for deepening our understanding this problem, which is not only a matter of doctrine, but also of pastoral priority in the modern era.

Introduction

1. St Peter encourages Christians to be always ready to give an account of the hope that is in them (cf. 1 *P* 3:15-16).[1] This document deals with the hope that Christians can have for the salvation of unbaptised infants who die. It indicates how such a hope has developed in recent decades and what its grounds are, so as to enable an account of that hope to be given. Though at first sight this topic may seem to be peripheral to theological concerns, questions of great depth and complexity are involved in its proper explication, and such an explication is called for today by pressing pastoral needs.

2. In these times, the number of infants who die unbaptised is growing greatly. This is partly because of parents, influenced by cultural relativism and religious pluralism, who are non-practising, but it is also partly a consequence of *in vitro* fertilisation and abortion. Given these developments, the question of the destiny of such infants is raised with new urgency. In such a situation, the ways by which salvation may be achieved appear ever more complex and problematic. The Church, faithful guardian of the way of salvation, knows that salvation can be achieved only in Christ, by the Holy Spirit. Yet, as mother and teacher, she cannot fail to reflect on the destiny of all human beings, created in the image of God,[2] and especially of the weakest. Being endowed with reason, conscience and freedom, adults are responsible for their own destiny in so far as they accept or reject God's grace. Infants, however, who do not yet have the use of reason, conscience and freedom, cannot decide for themselves. Parents experience great grief and feelings of guilt when they do not have the moral assurance of the salvation of their children, and people find it increasingly difficult to accept that God is just and merciful if he excludes infants, who have no personal sins, from eternal happiness, whether they are Christian or non-Christian. From a theological point of view, the development of a theology of hope and an ecclesiology of communion, together with

---

[1] All Scriptural references in this document are to the Revised Standard Version of the Bible (Catholic Edition).

[2] Cf. INTERNATIONAL THEOLOGICAL COMMISSION, *Communion and Stewardship: Human Persons Created in the Image of God*, Vatican City, 2005.

a recognition of the greatness of divine mercy, challenge an unduly restrictive view of salvation. In fact, the universal salvific will of God and the correspondingly universal mediation of Christ mean that all theological notions that ultimately call into question the very omnipotence of God, and his mercy in particular, are inadequate.

3. The idea of Limbo, which the Church has used for many centuries to designate the destiny of infants who die without Baptism, has no clear foundation in revelation, even though it has long been used in traditional theological teaching. Moreover, the notion that infants who die without Baptism are deprived of the beatific vision, which has for so long been regarded as the common doctrine of the Church, gives rise to numerous pastoral problems, so much so that many pastors of souls have asked for a deeper reflection on the ways of salvation. The necessary reconsideration of the theological issues cannot ignore the tragic consequences of original sin. Original sin implies a state of separation from Christ, and that excludes the possibility of the vision of God for those who die in that state.

4. Reflecting on the question of the destiny of infants who die without Baptism, the ecclesial community must keep in mind the fact that God is more properly the subject than the object of theology. The first task of theology is therefore to listen to the Word of God. Theology listens to the Word of God expressed in the Scriptures in order to communicate it lovingly to all people. However, with regard to the salvation of those who die without Baptism, the Word of God says little or nothing. It is therefore necessary to interpret the reticence of Scripture on this issue in the light of texts concerning the universal plan of salvation and the ways of salvation. In short, the problem both for theology and for pastoral care is how to safeguard and reconcile two sets of biblical affirmations: those concerning God's universal salvific will (cf. 1 *Tm* 2:4) and those regarding the necessity of Baptism as the way of being freed from sin and conformed to Christ (cf. *Mk* 16:16; *Mt* 28:18-19).

5. Secondly, taking account of the principle *lex orandi lex credendi*, the Christian community notes that there is no mention of Limbo in the liturgy. In fact, the liturgy contains a feast of the Holy Innocents,

who are venerated as martyrs, even though they were not baptised, because they were killed "on account of Christ".[3] There has even been an important liturgical development through the introduction of funerals for infants who died without Baptism. We do not pray for those who are damned. The *Roman Missal* of 1970 introduced a Funeral Mass for unbaptised infants whose parents intended to present them for Baptism. The Church entrusts to God's mercy those infants who die unbaptised. In its 1980 *Instruction on Children's Baptism*, the Congregation for the Doctrine of the Faith reaffirmed that: "with regard to children who die without having received Baptism, the Church can only entrust them to the mercy of God, as indeed she does in the funeral rite established for them".[4] The *Catechism of the Catholic Church* (1992) adds that: "the great mercy of God who desires that all men should be saved [1 *Tm* 2:4], and Jesus' tenderness toward children which caused him to say: 'Let the children come to me, do not hinder them' (*Mk* 10:14), allow us to hope that there is a way of salvation for children who have died without Baptism".[5]

6. Thirdly, the Church cannot fail to encourage the hope of salvation for infants who die without Baptism by the very fact that she "prays that no one should be lost",[6] and prays in hope for "all to be saved".[7] On the basis of an anthropology of solidarity,[8] strengthened by an ecclesial understanding of corporate personality, the Church knows the help that can be given by the faith of believers. The Gospel of Mark actually describes an occasion when the faith of some was effective for the salvation of another (cf. *Mk* 2:5). So, while knowing that the normal way to achieve salvation in Christ is by Baptism *in re*, the Church hopes that there may be other ways to achieve the same end. Because, by his Incarnation, the Son of God

---

[3] "Bethlehem, do not be sad, but be of good heart at the killing of the holy infants, because they were offered as perfect victims to Christ the King: having been sacrificed on account of him, they will reign with him", *Exapostilarion* of Matins in the Byzantine Liturgy, *Anthologion di tutto l'anno*, vol. 1, Edizione Lipa, Rome 1999, 1199.

[4] CONGREGATION FOR THE DOCTRINE OF THE FAITH, *Pastoralis actio*, n.13, *Acta Apostolicae Sedis* 72 (1980), 1144.

[5] *Catechism of the Catholic Church* (hereafter referred to as *CCC*), 1261.

[6] *CCC* 1058.

[7] *CCC* 1821.

[8] Cf. Gn 22:18; Ws 8:1; Ac 14:17; Rm 2:6-7; 1 Tm 2:4; *Synod of Quiercy*, DENZINGER Henricus and SCHÖNMETZER Adolfus (eds.), *Enchiridion Symbolorum Definitionum et Declarationum de rebus fidei et morum* (hereafter referred to as *DS*), Rome: Herder, 1976, 623; also *NA* 1.

"in a certain way united himself" with every human being, and because Christ died for all and all are in fact "called to one and the same destiny, which is divine", the Church believes that "the Holy Spirit offers to all the possibility of being made partners, in a way known to God, in the paschal mystery" (*GS* 22).[9]

7. Finally, when reflecting theologically on the salvation of infants who die without Baptism, the Church respects the hierarchy of truths and therefore begins by clearly reaffirming the primacy of Christ and his grace, which has priority over Adam and sin. Jesus Christ, in his existence for us and in the redemptive power of his sacrifice, died and rose again for all. By his whole life and teaching, he revealed the fatherhood of God and his universal love. While the necessity of Baptism is *de fide*, the tradition and the documents of the magisterium which have reaffirmed this necessity need to be interpreted. While it is true that the universal salvific will of God is not opposed to the necessity of Baptism, it is also true that infants, for their part, do not place any personal obstacle in the way of redemptive grace. On the other hand, Baptism is administered to infants, who are free from personal sins, not only in order to free them from original sin, but also to insert them into the communion of salvation which is the Church, by means of communion in the death and resurrection of Christ (cf. *Rm* 6:1-7). Grace is totally free, because it is always a pure gift of God. Damnation, however, is deserved, because it is the consequence of free human choice.[10] The infant who dies with Baptism is saved by the grace of Christ and through the intercession of the Church, even without his or her cooperation. It can be asked whether the infant who dies without Baptism, but for whom the Church in its prayer expresses the desire for salvation, can be deprived of the vision of God even without his or her cooperation.

---

[9] All references in English to the documents of Vatican II have been taken from Austin FLANNERY (General ed.), *Vatican II. The Conciliar and Post Conciliar Documents*, Dublin: Costello Publishing Company, 1975.

[10] Cf. *Synod of Quiercy*, *DS* 623.

1. *Historia Quaestionis*
History and Hermeneutics of Catholic Teaching

1.1. Biblical Foundations

8. A sound theological enquiry should start with a study of the biblical foundations of any ecclesial doctrine or practice. Hence, as regards the issue under discussion, the question should be asked whether the Holy Scriptures deal in one way or another with the question of the destiny of unbaptised children. Even a quick look through the New Testament, however, makes it clear that the early Christian communities were not yet confronted with the question whether infants or children who had died without Baptism would receive God's salvation. When the New Testament mentions the practice of Baptism, it generally points to the Baptism of adults. But the New Testament evidence does not preclude the possibility of infants being baptised. In households (*oikos*) where Baptism is mentioned in the Book of Acts 16:15 and 33 (cf. 18:8) and 1 Co 1:16, children may have been baptised along with adults. The absence of positive evidence may be explained by the fact that the New Testament writings are concerned mainly with the initial spread of Christianity in the world.

9. The lack of any positive teaching within the New Testament with respect to the destiny of unbaptised children does not mean that the theological discussion of this question is not informed by a number of fundamental biblical doctrines. These include:

(i) God wills to save all people (cf. *Gn* 3:15; 22:18; 1 *Tm* 2:3-6), through Jesus Christ's victory over sin and death (cf. *Ep* 1:20-22; *Ph* 2:7-11; *Rm* 14:9; 1 *Co* 15:20-28);

(ii) the universal sinfulness of human beings (cf. *Gn* 6:5-6; 8:21; 1 *K* 8:46; *Ps* 130:3), and their being born in sin (cf. *Ps* 51:7; *Si* 25:24) since Adam, and therefore their being destined to death (cf. *Rm* 5:12; 1 *Co* 15:22);

(iii) the necessity, for salvation, of the faith of the believer (cf. *Rm* 1:16), on the one hand, and of Baptism (cf. *Mk* 16:16; *Mt* 28:19; *Ac* 2:40-41; 16:30-33) and the Eucharist (cf. *Jn* 6:53) administered by the Church, on the other hand;

(iv) Christian hope goes utterly beyond human hope (cf. *Rm* 4:18-21); Christian hope is that the living God, the Saviour of all humanity (cf. 1 *Tm* 4:10) will share his glory with all people and that all will live with Christ (cf. 1 *Th* 5:9-11; *Rm* 8:2-5.23-25), and Christians must be ready to give an account of the hope they have (cf. 1 *P* 3:15);

(v) the Church must make "supplications, prayers and intercessions … for all" (1 *Tm* 2:1-8), based on faith that for God's creative power "nothing is impossible" (*Jb* 42:2; *Mk* 10:27; 12:24.27; *Lk* 1:37), and on the hope that the whole creation will finally share in the glory of God (cf. *Rm* 8:22-27).

10. There seems to be a tension between two of the biblical doctrines just mentioned: the universal salvific will of God on the one side, and the necessity of sacramental Baptism on the other. The latter seems to limit the extension of God's universal salvific will. Hence a hermeneutical reflection is needed about how the witnesses of tradition (Church Fathers, the magisterium, theologians) read and used biblical texts and doctrines with respect to the problem being dealt with. More specifically, one has to clarify what kind of 'necessity' is claimed with respect to the sacrament of Baptism in order to avoid a mistaken understanding. The necessity of sacramental Baptism is a necessity of the second order compared to the absolute necessity of God's saving act through Jesus Christ for the final salvation of every human being. Sacramental Baptism is necessary because it is the ordinary means through which a person shares the beneficial effects of Jesus' death and resurrection. In what follows, we will be attentive to the way scriptural witnesses have been used in the tradition. Moreover, in dealing with theological principles (Chapter 2) and with our reasons for hope (Chapter 3), we will discuss in greater detail the biblical doctrines and texts involved.

1.2. The Greek Fathers

11. Very few Greek Fathers dealt with the destiny of infants who die without Baptism because there was no controversy about this issue in the East. Furthermore, they had a different view of the present condition of humanity. For the Greek Fathers, as the consequence of Adam's sin, human beings inherited corruption, possibility,

and mortality, from which they could be restored by a process of deification made possible through the redemptive work of Christ. The idea of an inheritance of sin or guilt - common in Western tradition - was foreign to this perspective, since in their view sin could only be a free, personal act.[11] Hence, not many Greek Fathers explicitly deal with the problem of the salvation of unbaptised children. They do, however, discuss the status or situation - but not the place - of these infants after their death. In this regard, the main problem they face is the tension between God's universal salvific will and the teaching of the Gospel about the necessity of Baptism. Pseudo-Athanasios says clearly that an unbaptised person cannot enter the Kingdom of God. He also asserts that unbaptised children will not enter the Kingdom, but neither will they be lost, for they have not sinned.[12] Anastasius of Sinai expresses this even more clearly: for him, unbaptised children do not go to Gehenna. But he is not able to say more; he does not express an opinion about where they do go, but leaves their destiny to God's judgment.[13]

12. Alone among the Greek Fathers, Gregory of Nyssa wrote a work specifically on the destiny of infants who die, *De infantibus praemature abreptis libellum*.[14] The anguish of the Church appears in the questions he puts to himself: the destiny of these infants is a mystery, "something much greater than the human mind can grasp".[15] He expresses his opinion in relation to virtue and its reward; in his view, there is no reason for God to grant what is hoped for as a reward. Virtue is not worth anything if those who depart this life prematurely without having practised virtue are immediately welcomed into blessedness. Continuing along this line, Gregory asks: "What will happen to the one who finishes his life at a tender age, who has done nothing, bad or good? Is he

[11] Cf. D. WEAVER, "The Exegesis of Romans 5:12 among the Greek Fathers and its Implication for the Doctrine of Original Sin: The 5th – 12th Centuries", *St Vladimir's Theological Quarterly* 29 (1985), 133-159, 231-257.

[12] (PSEUDO-) ATHANASIOS, *Quaestiones ad Antiochum ducem*, qn. 101 (*Patrologia cursus completa, series graeca* [PG], J.P. MIGNE (ed.), 28, 660C). Likewise qn. 115 (PG 28, 672A).

[13] ANASTASIUS OF SINAI, *Quaestiones et responsiones*, qn. 81 (PG 89, 709C).

[14] *De infantibus praemature abreptis libellum, ab H. POLACK ad editionem praeparatum in Colloquio Leidensi testimoniis instructum renovatis curis recensitum edendum curavit Hadwiga HÖRNER, in J. K. DOWNING – J. A. McDONOUGH – H. HÖRNER (ed. cur.), Gregorii Nysseni opera dogmatica minora, Pars II , W. JAEGER – H. LANGERBECK – H. HÖRNER (eds.), Gregorii Nysseni opera, Volumen III, Pars II*, Leiden – New York – København – Köln 1987, 65-97.

[15] *Ibid.*, 70.

worthy of a reward?"[16] He answers: "The hoped-for blessedness belongs to human beings by nature, and it is called a reward only in a certain sense".[17] Enjoyment of true life (*zoe* and not *bios*) corresponds to human nature, and is possessed in the degree that virtue is practised. Since the innocent infant does not need purification from personal sins, he shares in this life corresponding to his nature in a sort of regular progress, according to his capacity. Gregory of Nyssa distinguishes between the destiny of infants and that of adults who lived a virtuous life. "The premature death of newborn infants does not provide a basis for the presupposition that they will suffer torments or that they will be in the same state as those who have been purified in this life by all the virtues".[18] Finally, he offers this perspective for the reflection of the Church: "Apostolic contemplation fortifies our inquiry, for the One who has done everything well, with wisdom (*Ps* 104: 24), is able to bring good out of evil".[19]

13. Gregory of Nazianzus does not write about the place and status after death of infants who die without sacramental Baptism, but he enlarges the subject with another consideration. He writes, namely, that these children receive neither praise nor punishment from the Just Judge, because they have suffered injury rather than provoked it. "The one who does not deserve punishment is not thereby worthy of praise, and the one who does not deserve praise is not thereby deserving of punishment".[20] The profound teaching of the Greek Fathers can be summarized in the opinion of Anastasius of Sinai: "It would not be fitting to probe God's judgments with one's hands".[21]

14. On the one hand, these Greek Fathers teach that children who die without Baptism do not suffer eternal damnation, though they do not attain the same state as those who have been baptised. On the other hand, they do not explain what their state is like or where they go. In this matter, the Greek Fathers display their characteristic apophatic sensitivity.

---

[16] *Ibid.*, 81-82.
[17] *Ibid.*, 83.
[18] *Ibid.*, 96.
[19] *Ibid.*, 97.
[20] GREGORY OF NAZIANZUS, *Oratio XL — In sanctum baptisma*, 23 (PG 36, 389B-C).
[21] ANASTASIUS OF SINAI, *Quaestiones et responsiones*, qn. 81 (PG 89, 709C).

1.3. The Latin Fathers

15. The fate of unbaptised infants first became the subject of sustained theological reflection in the West during the anti-Pelagian controversies of the early 5th century. St Augustine addressed the question because Pelagius was teaching that infants could be saved without Baptism. Pelagius questioned whether St Paul's letter to the Romans really taught that all human beings sinned "in Adam" (*Rm* 5:12) and that concupiscence, suffering, and death were a consequence of the Fall.[22] Since he denied that Adam's sin was transmitted to his descendants, he regarded newborn infants as innocent. Pelagius promised infants who died unbaptised entry into "eternal life" (not, however, into the "Kingdom of God" [*Jn* 3:5]), reasoning that God would not condemn to hell those who were not personally guilty of sin.[23]

16. In countering Pelagius, Augustine was led to state that infants who die without Baptism are consigned to hell.[24] He appealed to the Lord's precept, John 3:5, and to the Church's liturgical practice. Why are little children brought to the baptismal font, especially infants in danger of death, if not to assure them entrance into the Kingdom of God? Why are they subjected to exorcisms and exsufflations if they do not have to be delivered from the devil?[25] Why are they born again if they do not need to be made new? Liturgical practice confirms the Church's belief that all inherit Adam's sin and must be transferred from the power of darkness into the kingdom of light (*Col* 1:13).[26] There is only one Baptism, the same for infants and adults, and it is for the forgiveness of sins.[27] If little children are baptized, then, it is because they are sinners. Although they clearly are not guilty of personal sin, according to

---

[22] Cf. PELAGIUS, *Expositio in epistolam ad Romanos*, in *Expositiones XIII epistolarum Pauli*, A. SOUTER (ed.), Cambridge, 1926.

[23] Cf. AUGUSTINE, *Epistula* 156, *Corpus scriptorum ecclesiasticorum latinorum* (hereafter CSEL), 44, 448f.; 175.6 (CSEL 44, 660-62); 176.3, (CSEL 44, 666f.); *De peccatorum meritis et remissione et de baptismo parvulorum* 1.20.26; 3. 5.11-6.12 (CSEL 60, 25f. and 137 – 139); *De gestis Pelagii* 11, 23-24 (CSEL 42, 76-78).

[24] Cf. *De pecc. mer.* 1.16.21 (CSEL 60, 20f.) ; *Sermo* 294.3, *Patrologia cursus completa, series latina* (PL), J.P. MIGNE (ed.), 38, 1337; *Contra Iulianum* 5.11.44 (PL 44, 809).

[25] Cf. *De pecc. mer.* 1.34.63 (CSEL 60, 63f.).

[26] Cf. *De gratia Christi et de peccato originali* 2.40.45 (CSEL 42, 202f.); *De nuptiis et concupiscentia* 2.18.33 (CSEL 42, 286f.).

[27] Cf. *Sermo* 293.11 (PL 38, 1334).

Romans 5:12 (in the Latin translation available to Augustine), they have sinned "in Adam".[28] "Why did Christ die for them if they are not guilty?"[29] All need Christ as their Saviour.

17. In Augustine's judgement, Pelagius undermined belief in Jesus Christ, the one Mediator (1 *Tm* 2:5), and in the need for the saving grace he won for us on the Cross. Christ came to save sinners. He is the "Great Physician" who offers even infants the medicine of Baptism to save them from the inherited sin of Adam.[30] The sole remedy for the sin of Adam, passed on to everyone through human generation, is Baptism. Those who are not baptized cannot enter the Kingdom of God. At the judgement, those who do not enter the Kingdom (*Mt* 25:34) will be condemned to hell (*Mt* 25:41). There is no "middle ground" between heaven and hell. "There is no middle place left, where you can put babies".[31] Anyone "who is not with Christ must be with the devil".[32]

18. God is just. If he condemns unbaptised children to hell, it is because they are sinners. Although these infants are punished in hell, they will suffer only the "mildest condemnation" ("*mitissima poena*"),[33] "the lightest punishment of all",[34] for there are diverse punishments in proportion to the guilt of the sinner.[35] These infants were unable to help themselves, but there is no injustice in their condemnation because all belong to "the same mass", the mass destined for perdition. God does no injustice to those who are not elected, for all deserve hell.[36] Why is it that some are vessels of wrath and others vessels of mercy? Augustine admits that he "cannot find a satisfactory and worthy explanation". He can only exclaim with St Paul: "How inscrutable [God's] judgments, and untraceable his ways!"[37] Rather than condemn divine authority, he gives a restrictive interpretation of God's universal salvific will.

---

[28] Cf. *De pecc. mer.* 1.9—15.20 (CSEL 60, 10-20).

[29] *"Cur ergo pro illis Christus mortuus est si non sunt rei?" in De nupt. et conc.* 2:33.56 (CSEL 42, 513).

[30] Cf. *Sermo* 293.8-11 (PL 38, 1333f.).

[31] *Sermo* 294.3 (PL 38, 1337).

[32] *De pecc. mer.* 1.28.55 (CSEL 60, 54).

[33] *Enchiridion ad Laurentium* 93 (PL 40, 275); cf. *De pecc. mer.* 1.16.21 (CSEL 60, 20f.).

[34] *C. Iul.* 5.11.44 (PL 44, 809).

[35] Cf. *Contra Iulianum opus imperfectum* 4.122 (CSEL 85, 141 – 142).

[36] *Contra duas Epistulas Pelagianorum* 2.7.13 (CSEL 60, 474).

[37] *Sermo* 294.7.7 (PL 38, 1339).

The Church believes that if anyone is redeemed, it is only by God's unmerited mercy; but if anyone is condemned, it is by his well-merited judgment. We shall discover the justice of God's will in the next world.[38]

19. The Council of Carthage of 418 rejected the teaching of Pelagius. It condemned the opinion that infants "do not contract from Adam any trace of original sin, which must be expiated by the bath of regeneration that leads to eternal life". Positively, this council taught that "even children who of themselves cannot have yet committed any sin are truly baptised for the remission of sins, so that by regeneration they may be cleansed from what they contracted through generation".[39] It was also added that there is no "intermediate or other happy dwelling place for children who have left this life without Baptism, without which they cannot enter the kingdom of heaven, that is, eternal life".[40] This council did not, however, explicitly endorse all aspects of Augustine's stern view about the destiny of infants who die without Baptism.

20. So great was Augustine's authority in the West, however, that the Latin Fathers (e.g., Jerome, Fulgentius, Avitus of Vienne, and Gregory the Great) did adopt his opinion. Gregory the Great asserts that God condemns even those with only original sin on their souls; even infants who have never sinned by their own will must go to "everlasting torments". He cites Job 14:4-5 (LXX), John 3:5, and Ephesians 2:3 on our condition at birth as "children of wrath".[41]

---

[38] Cf. *Enchir.* 94-95 (PL 40, 275f.); *De nat. et grat.* 3.3-5.5 (PL 44, 249f.).

[39] *DS* 223. This teaching was adopted by the Council of Trent. COUNCIL OF TRENT, Fifth Session, Decree on Original Sin, *DS* 1514; J. NEUNER – J. DUPUIS (eds.), *The Christian Faith in the Doctrinal Documents of the Catholic Church,* Theological Publications in India, Bangalore 2004 (hereafter referred to as *ND*), 511.

[40] *DS*, 224: *"Item placuit, ut si quis dicit, ideo dixisse Dominum: 'In domo Patris mei mansiones multae sunt (Io 14,2), ut intelligatur, quia in regno caelorum erit aliquis medius aut ullus alicubi locus, ubi beati vivant parvuli, qui sine baptismo ex hac vita migrarunt, sine quo in regno caelorum, quod est vita aeterna, intrare non possunt, anathema sit".* Cf. *Concilia Africae A. 345 – A. 525*, C. MUNIER (ed.), Turnhout: Brepols, 1974, 70. This canon is found in some manuscripts, but it is missing from others. The *Indiculus* did not take it up. Cf. *DS* 238 – 249; *ND* 1907 - 1914.

[41] GREGORY THE GREAT, *Moralia,* 9.21, commenting on Job 9:17 (PL 75, 877). See also *Moralia,* 12.9 (PL 75, 992-993) and 13.44 (PL 75, 1038).

1.4. The Medieval Scholastics

21. Augustine was the point of reference for Latin theologians throughout the Middle Ages on this matter. Anselm of Canterbury is a good example: he believes that little children who die without Baptism are damned on account of original sin and in keeping with God's justice.[42] The common doctrine was summarized by Hugh of St Victor: infants who die unbaptised cannot be saved because (1) they have not received the sacrament, and (2) they cannot make a personal act of faith that would supply for the sacrament.[43] This doctrine implies that one needs to be justified during one's earthly life in order to enter eternal life after death. Death puts an end to the possibility of choosing to accept or reject grace, that is, to adhere to God or turn away from him; after death, a person's fundamental dispositions before God receive no further modification.

22. But most of the later medieval authors, from Peter Abelard on, underline the goodness of God and interpret Augustine's "mildest punishment" as the privation of the beatific vision (*carentia visionis Dei*), without hope of obtaining it, but with no additional penalties.[44] This teaching, which modified the strict opinion of St Augustine, was disseminated by Peter Lombard: little children suffer no penalty except the privation of the vision of God.[45] This position led the theological reflection of the thirteenth century to assign unbaptised infants a destiny essentially different from that of the saints in heaven, but also partly different from that of the reprobate, with whom they are nonetheless associated. This did not prevent the medieval theologians from holding the existence of two (and not three) possible outcomes for human existence: the happiness of heaven for the saints, and the privation of this celestial happiness for the damned and for infants who died unbaptised. In the developments of medieval doctrine, the loss of the Beatific Vision (*poena damni*) was understood to be the proper punishment for original sin, whereas the "torments of perpetual hell" constituted

---

[42] Cf. *De conceptu virginali et de originali peccato*, F.S. SCHMITT (ed.), t. II, cap. 28, 170-171.

[43] Cf. *Summa Sententiarum, tract.* V, *cap.* 6 (PL 176, 132).

[44] Cf. Peter ABELARD, *Commentaria in Epistolam Pauli ad Romanos*, Liber II [5,19] (*Corpus Christianorum, Continuatio Mediaevalis* 11), 169-170.

[45] Cf. *Sententiae*, Lib. II, dist. 33, cap. 2, I. BRADY (ed.), t. I/2, Grottaferrata 1971, 520.

the punishment for mortal sins actually committed.[46] In the Middle Ages, the ecclesiastical magisterium affirmed more than once that those "who die in mortal sin" and those who die "with original sin only" receive "different punishments".[47]

23. Because children below the age of reason did not commit actual sin, theologians came to the common view that these unbaptised children feel no pain at all, or even that they enjoy a full natural happiness through their union with God in all natural goods (Thomas Aquinas, Duns Scotus).[48] The contribution of this last theological thesis consists especially in its recognition of an authentic joy among children who die without sacramental Baptism: they possess a true form of union with God proportionate to their condition. The thesis relies on a certain way of conceptualising the relationship between the natural and the supernatural orders, and, in particular, the orientation to the supernatural; it must not be confused, however, with the later development of the idea of "pure nature". Thomas Aquinas, for instance, insisted that faith alone allows us to know that the supernatural end of human life consists in the glory of the saints, that is, in participation in the life of the Triune God through the beatific vision. Since this supernatural end transcends natural human knowledge, and since unbaptised children lack the sacrament that would have given them the seed of such supernatural knowledge, Aquinas concluded that infants who die without Baptism do not know what they are deprived of, and hence do not suffer from the privation of the beatific vision.[49] Even when they adopted such a view, theologians considered the privation of the beatific vision as an affliction ("punishment") within the divine economy. The theological doctrine of a "natural beatitude" (and

[46] Cf. INNOCENT III, Letter to Humbert, Archbishop of Arles "Maiores Ecclesiae causas" (*DS* 780): *"Poena originalis peccati est carentia visionis Dei, actualis vero poena peccati est gehennae perpetuae cruciatus..."* This theological tradition identified the "torments of hell" with afflictive pains both sensible and spiritual; cf. Thomas AQUINAS, *IV Sent.*, dist. 44, q. 3, a. 3, qla 3; dist. 50, q. 2, a. 3.

[47] COUNCIL OF LYONS II, *Profession of Faith for Michael Paleologus*, *DS* 858; JOHN XXII, Letter to the Armenians *"Nequaquam sine dolore"*, *DS* 926; COUNCIL OF FLORENCE, Decree: *"Laetentur Caeli"*, *DS* 1306.

[48] Thomas AQUINAS, *II Sent.*, dist. 33, q. 2, a. 2; *De malo*, q. 5, a. 3. John DUNS SCOTUS, *Lectura* II, dist. 33, q. un.; *Ordinatio* II, dist. 33, q. un.

[49] Thomas AQUINAS, *De malo*, q. 5, a. 3: *"Anime puerorum...carent supernaturali cognitione que hic in nobis per fidem plantatur, eo quod nec hic fidem habuerunt in actu, nec sacramentum fidei susceperunt... Et ideo se privari tali bono anime puerorum non cognoscunt, et propter hoc non dolent"*. Cf. *ibid.*, ad 4; Leonine edition, vol. 23, 136.

the absence of any suffering) can be understood as an attempt to account for God's justice and mercy regarding children who did not commit any actual fault, thus giving more weight to God's mercy than in Augustine's view. The theologians who held this thesis of a natural happiness for children who died without Baptism manifest a very lively sense of the gratuity of salvation and of the mystery of God's will that human thought cannot fully grasp.

24. The theologians who taught, in one form or another, that unbaptised children are deprived of the vision of God generally held at the same time a double affirmation: (a) God wills that everyone be saved, and (b) God, who wills that all be saved, wills equally the dispensations and the means that he himself has established for this salvation and that he has made known to us by his revelation. The second affirmation, of itself, does not exclude other dispositions of the divine economy (as is clear, for example, in the witness of the Holy Innocents). As for the expression "Limbo of Infants", it was forged at the turn of the 12th-13th century to name the "resting place" of such infants (the "border" of the inferior region). Theologians could discuss this question, however, without using the word "Limbo". Their doctrines should not be confused with the use of the word "Limbo".

25. The main affirmation of these doctrines is that those who were not capable of a free act by which they could consent to grace, and who died without having been regenerated by the sacrament of Baptism, are deprived of the vision of God because of original sin which they inherit through human generation.

1.5. The Modern/Post-Tridentine Era

26. Augustine's thought enjoyed a revival in the 16th century, and with it his theory regarding the fate of unbaptised infants, as Robert Bellarmine, for example, bears witness.[50] One consequence of this revival of Augustinianism was Jansenism. Together with Catholic theologians of the Augustinian school, the Jansenists vigorously opposed the theory of Limbo. During this period the popes (Paul III,

[50] Cf. Robert BELLARMINE, *De amissione gratiae* VI, c.2 and c.6, in *Opera*, vol. 5, Paris: Vivès, 1873, 458, 470.

Benedict XIV, Clement XIII)[51] defended the right of Catholics to teach Augustine's stern view that infants dying with original sin alone are damned and punished with the perpetual torment of the fire of hell, though with the "mildest pain" (Augustine) compared with what was suffered by adults who were punished for their mortal sins. On the other hand, when the Jansenist Synod of Pistoia (1786) denounced the medieval theory of "Limbo", Pius VI defended the right of the Catholic Schools to teach that those who died with the guilt of original sin alone are punished with the lack of the Beatific Vision ("punishment of loss"), but not sensible pains (the punishment of "fire"). In the bull "Auctorem Fidei" (1794), the Pope condemned as "false, rash, injurious to the Catholic schools" the Jansenist teaching "which rejects as a Pelagian fable [*fabula pelagiana*] that place in the lower regions (which the faithful call the 'Limbo of Children') in which the souls of those departing with the sole guilt of original sin are punished with the punishment of the condemned, without the punishment of fire, just as if whoever removes the punishment of fire thereby introduces that middle place and state free of guilt and of punishment between the Kingdom of God and eternal damnation of which the Pelagians idly talk".[52] Papal interventions during this period, then, protected the freedom of the Catholic schools to wrestle with this question. They did not endorse the theory of Limbo as a doctrine of faith. Limbo, however, was the common Catholic teaching until the mid-20th century.

1.6. From the Time of Vatican I to Vatican II

27. Prior to the First Vatican Council, and again prior to the Second Vatican Council, there was a strong interest in some quarters in defining Catholic doctrine on this matter. This interest was evident

[51] Cf. PAUL III, "Alias cum felicitate" (23 September 1535), in JO. LAURENTII BERTI FLORENTINI, *Opus de theologicis disciplinis*, Venetiis: Ex Typographia Remondiniana, 1760, vol. V, 36; PAUL III, "Cum alias quorumdam" (11 March 1538), in *ibid*., vol. I, 167-68; BENEDICT XIV, "Dum praeterito mense" (31 July 1748), "Non sine magno" (30 December 1750), "Sotto il 15 di luglio" (12 May 1751), in *Benedicti XIV Acta sive nondum sive sparsim edita nunc autem primum collecta cura Raphaelis de Martinis*, Neapoli, Ex Typogr. Puerorum Artificium, 1894, vol. I, 554-57; vol. II, 74, 412-413. For other texts and references, see G. J. DYER, *The Denial of Limbo and the Jansenist Controversy*, Mundelein, IL: Saint Mary of the Lake Seminary, 1955, 139-59; see especially on pp, 139-142, the account of the discussions under Clement XIII in 1758 – 1759, according to the manuscript 1485 of the *Biblioteca Corsiniana*, Rome, classification mark 41.C.15 ("Cause trattate nella S. C. del Sant`Uffizio di Roma dal 1733 al 1761").

[52] PIUS VI, Bull "Auctorem Fidei", *DS* 2626. On this question, see G. J. DYER, *The Denial of Limbo and the Jansenist Controversy*, 159 - 170.

in the revised schema of the dogmatic constitution, *De doctrina catholica*, prepared for the First Vatican Council (but not voted upon by the Council), which presented the destiny of children who died without Baptism as between that of the damned, on the one hand, and that of the souls in purgatory and the blessed, on the other: *"Etiam qui cum solo originali peccato mortem obeunt, beata Dei visione in perpetuum carebunt"*.[53] In the 20th century, however, theologians sought the right to imagine new solutions, including the possibility that Christ's full salvation reaches these infants.[54]

28. In the preparatory phase of Vatican II, there was a desire on the part of some that the Council affirm the common doctrine that unbaptised infants cannot attain the Beatific Vision, and thereby close the question. The Central Preparatory Commission, which was aware of many arguments against the traditional doctrine and of the need to propose a solution in better accordance with the developing *sensus fidelium*, opposed this move. Because it was thought that theological reflection on the issue was not mature enough, the question was not included in the Council's agenda; it did not enter into the Council's deliberations and was left open for further investigation.[55] The question raised a number of problems whose outcome was debated among theologians, in particular: the status of the Church's traditional teaching concerning children who die without Baptism; the absence of an explicit indication in Holy Scripture on the subject; the connection between the natural order and the supernatural vocation of human beings; original sin

---

[53] *Schema reformatum constitutionis dogmaticae de doctrina catholica*, cap. V, n. 6 in *Acta et Decreta Sacrorum Conciliorum Recentiorum, Collectio Lacensis*, t. 7, Friburgi Brisgoviae 1890, 565.

[54] For a survey of the discussions and of some new solutions proposed before Vatican II, see Y. CONGAR, *"Morts avant l'aurore de la raison"*, in *Vaste monde ma paroisse: Vérité et dimensions du Salut*, Paris: Témoignage Chrétien, 1959, 174-183; G. DYER, *Limbo: Unsettled Question*, New York: Sheed and Ward 1964, 93-182 (with the indication of many publications on pp. 192-196); W. A. van ROO, "Infants Dying without Baptism: A Survey of Recent Literature and Determination of the State of the Question", *Gregorianum* 35 (1954), 406-473; A. MICHEL, *Enfants morts sans baptême*, Paris: Téqui, 1954; C. JOURNET, *La volonté divine salvifique sur les petits enfants*, Paris: Desclée de Brouwer 1958; L. RENWART, *"Le baptême des enfants et les limbes"*, *Nouvelle Revue Théologique* 80 (1958), 449-467; H. de LAVALETTE, *"Autour de la question des enfants morts sans baptême"*, *Nouvelle Revue Théologique* 82 (1960), 56-69; P. GUMPEL, "Unbaptized Infants: May They be Saved?", *The Downside Review*, 72 (1954), 342-458; IDEM, "Unbaptized Infants: A Further Report", *The Downside Review* 73 (1955), 317-346; V. WILKIN, *From Limbo to Heaven: An Essay on the Economy of Redemption*, New York: Sheed and Ward, 1961. After Vatican II: E. BOISSARD, *Réflexions sur le sort des enfants morts sans baptême*, Paris: Éditions de la Source, 1974.

[55] For the references, see G. ALBERIGO and J.A. KOMONCHAK (eds.), *History of Vatican II*, vol. 1, Maryknoll: Orbis & Leuven: Peeters, 1995, 236-245; 308-310.

and the universal saving will of God; and the "substitutions" for sacramental Baptism that can be invoked for young children.

29. The Catholic Church's belief that Baptism is necessary for salvation was powerfully expressed in the Decree for the Jacobites at the Council of Florence in 1442: "There is no other way to come to the aid [of little children] than the sacrament of Baptism by which they are snatched from the power of the devil and adopted as children of God".[56] This teaching implies a very vivid perception of the divine favour displayed in the sacramental economy instituted by Christ; the Church does not know of any other means which would certainly give little children access to eternal life. However, the Church has also traditionally recognized some substitutions for Baptism of water (which is the sacramental incorporation into the mystery of Christ dead and risen), namely, Baptism of blood (incorporation into Christ by witness of martyrdom for Christ) and Baptism of desire (incorporation into Christ by the desire or longing for sacramental Baptism). During the 20th century, some theologians, developing certain more ancient theological theses, proposed to recognize for little children either some kind of Baptism of blood (by taking into consideration the suffering and death of these infants), or some kind of Baptism of desire (by invoking an "unconscious desire" for Baptism in these infants oriented toward justification, or the desire of the Church).[57] The proposals invoking some kind of Baptism of desire or Baptism of blood, however, involved certain difficulties. On the one hand, the adult's act of desire for Baptism can hardly be attributed to children. The little child is scarcely capable of supplying the fully free and responsible personal act which would constitute a substitution for sacramental Baptism; such a fully free and responsible act is rooted in a judgement of reason and cannot be properly achieved before the human person has reached a sufficient or appropriate use of reason (*aetas discretionis*: "age of discretion"). On the other hand, it is difficult to understand how the Church could properly "supply" for unbaptised infants. The case of sacramental Baptism, instead, is quite different because sacramental Baptism, administered to infants, obtains grace in virtue of that which is specifically proper to the sacrament as such, that is, the certain gift of

---

[56] *DS* 1349.

[57] On these propositions and the questions they raised, see G. J. DYER, *The Denial of Limbo*, 102-122.

regeneration by the power of Christ himself. That is why Pope Pius XII, recalling the importance of sacramental Baptism, explained in the "Allocution to Italian Midwives" in 1951: "The state of grace is absolutely necessary for salvation: without it supernatural happiness, the beatific vision of God, cannot be attained. In an adult an act of love may suffice to obtain him sanctifying grace and so supply for the lack of Baptism; to the child still unborn, or newly born, this way is not open".[58] This gave rise among theologians to a renewed reflection on the dispositions of infants with respect to the reception of divine grace, on the possibility of an extra-sacramental configuration to Christ, and on the maternal mediation of the Church.

30. It is equally necessary to note, among the debated questions with a bearing on this matter, that of the gratuity of the supernatural order. Before the Second Vatican Council, in other circumstances and regarding other questions, Pius XII had vigorously brought this to the consciousness of the Church by explaining that one destroys the gratuity of the supernatural order if one asserts that God could not create intelligent beings without ordaining and calling them to the Beatific Vision.[59] The goodness and justice of God do not imply that grace is necessarily or "automatically" given. Among theologians, then, reflection on the destiny of unbaptised infants involved from that time onwards a renewed consideration of the absolute gratuity of grace, and of the ordination of all human beings to Christ and to the redemption that he won for us.

31. Without responding directly to the question of the destiny of unbaptised infants, the Second Vatican Council marked out many paths to guide theological reflection. The Council recalled many times the universality of God's saving will which extends to all people (1 *Tm* 2:4).[60] All "share a common destiny, namely God. His providence, evident goodness, and saving designs extend to all humankind" (*NA* 1, cf. *LG* 16). In a more particular vein, presenting a conception of human life founded on the dignity of the human being created in the image of God, the constitution *Gaudium et*

---

[58] PIUS XII, "Allocution to Italian Midwives", *Acta Apostolicae Sedis*, 43 (1951), 841.

[59] Cf. PIUS XII, Encyclical Letter *"Humani generis"*, *Acta Apostolicae Sedis*, 42 (1950), 570: *"Alii veram 'gratuitatem' ordinis supernaturalis corrumpunt, cum autument Deum entia intellectu praedita condere non posse, quin eadem ad beatificam visionem ordinet et vocet"*.

[60] Cf. *LG* 15-16; *NA* 1; *DH* 11; *AG* 7.

Spes recalls that, "[h]uman dignity rests above all on the fact that humanity is called to communion with God," specifying that "[t]he invitation to converse with God is addressed to men and women as soon as they are born" (*GS* 19). This same constitution proclaims with vigour that only in the mystery of the Incarnate Word does the mystery of the human being take on light. Furthermore, there is the renowned statement of the Council which asserted: "since Christ died for all, and since all are in fact called to one and the same destiny, which is divine, we must hold that the Holy Spirit offers to all the possibility of being made partners, in a way known to God, in the paschal mystery" (*GS* 22). Although the Council did not expressly apply this teaching to children who die without Baptism, these passages open a way to account for hope in their favour.[61]

1.7. Issues of a Hermeneutical Nature

32. The study of history shows an evolution and a development of Catholic teaching concerning the destiny of infants who die without Baptism. This progress engages some foundational doctrinal principles which remain permanent, and some secondary elements of unequal value. In effect, revelation does not communicate directly in an explicit fashion knowledge of God's plan for unbaptised children, but it enlightens the Church regarding the principles of faith which must guide her thought and her practice. A theological reading of the history of Catholic teaching up to Vatican II shows in particular that three main affirmations which belong to the faith of the Church appear at the core of the problem of the fate of unbaptised infants. (i) God wants all human beings to be saved. (ii) This salvation is given only through participation in Christ's paschal mystery, that is, through Baptism for the forgiveness of sins, either sacramental or in some other way. Human beings, including infants, cannot be saved apart from the grace of Christ poured out by the Holy Spirit. (iii) Infants will not enter the Kingdom of God without being freed from original sin by redemptive grace.

[61] See for instance – among other authors – the observations of K. RAHNER. *"Die bleibende Bedeutung des II Vatikanischen Konzils," Schriften zur Theologie*, Band XIV, Benziger Verlag: Zürich, Köln, Einsiedeln, 1980, 314-316. With other nuances: J.-H. NICOLAS, *Synthèse dogmatique. De la Trinité à la Trinité*, Fribourg, Paris: Editions Universitaires, Beauchesne, 1985, 848-853. See also the observations of J. Ratzinger speaking as a private theologian in: Vittorio MESSORI a colloquio con il cardinale Joseph RATZINGER, *Rapporto sulla fede*, Cinisello Balsamo: Edizioni Paoline, 1985, 154-155.

33. The history of theology and of magisterial teaching show in particular a development concerning the manner of understanding the universal saving will of God. The theological tradition of the past (antiquity, the Middle Ages, the beginning of modern times), in particular the Augustinian tradition, often presents what by comparison with modern theological developments would seem to be a "restrictive" conception of the universality of God's saving will.[62] In theological research, the perception of the divine will to save as "quantitatively" universal is relatively recent. At the level of the magisterium, this larger perception was progressively affirmed. Without trying to date it exactly, one can observe that it appeared very clearly in the 19th century, especially in the teaching of Pius IX on the possible salvation of those who, without fault on their part, were unaware of the Catholic faith: those who "lead a virtuous and just life, can, with the aid of divine light and grace, attain eternal life; for God, who understands perfectly, scrutinizes and knows the minds, souls, thoughts and habits of all, in his very great goodness and patience, will not permit anyone who is not guilty of a voluntary fault to be punished with eternal torments".[63] This integration and maturation in Catholic doctrine meanwhile gave rise to a renewed reflection on the possible ways of salvation for unbaptised infants.

34. In the Church's tradition, the affirmation that children who died unbaptised are deprived of the beatific vision has for a long time been "common doctrine". This common doctrine followed upon a certain way of reconciling the received principles of revelation, but it did not possess the certitude of a statement of faith, or the same certitude as other affirmations whose rejection would entail the denial of a divinely revealed dogma or of a teaching proclaimed by a definitive act of the magisterium. The study of the history of the Church's reflection on this subject shows that it is necessary to make distinctions. In this summary we distinguish first, statements of faith and what pertains to the faith; second, common doctrine; and third, theological opinion.

---

[62] See above, footnote 38.

[63] PIUS IX, Encyclical Letter *"Quanto conficiamur"*, 10.09.1863 (*DS* 2866): *"...qui...honestam rectamque vitam agunt, posse, divinae lucis et gratiae operante virtute, aeternam consequi vitam, cum Deus, qui omnium mentes, animos, cogitationes habitusque plane intuetur, scrutatur et noscit, pro summa sua bonitate et clementia minime patiatur, quempiam aeternis puniri suppliciis, qui voluntarie culpae reatum non habeat"*.

35. a) The Pelagian understanding of the access of unbaptised infants to "eternal life" must be considered as contrary to Catholic faith.

36. b) The affirmation that "the punishment for original sin is the loss of the beatific vision", formulated by Innocent III,[64] pertains to the faith: original sin is of itself an impediment to the beatific vision. Grace is necessary in order to be purified of original sin and to be raised to communion with God so as to be able to enter into eternal life and enjoy the vision of God. Historically, the common doctrine applied this affirmation to the fate of unbaptised infants and concluded that these infants lack the beatific vision. But Pope Innocent's teaching, in its content of faith, does not necessarily imply that infants who die without sacramental Baptism are deprived of grace and condemned to the loss of the beatific vision; it allows us to hope that God who wants all to be saved, provides some merciful remedy for their purification from original sin and their access to the beatific vision.

37. c) In the documents of the magisterium in the Middle Ages, the mention of "different punishments" for those who die in actual mortal sin or with original sin only ("As for the souls of those who die in mortal sin or with original sin only, they go down immediately to hell, to be punished, however, with different punishments")[65] must be interpreted according to the common teaching of the time. Historically, these affirmations have certainly been applied to unbaptised infants, with the conclusion that these infants suffer punishment for original sin. It must be observed however that, in a general way, the focus of these Church pronouncements was not on the lack of salvation for unbaptised infants, but on the immediacy of the particular judgment after death and the assignment of souls to heaven or hell. These magisterial statements do not oblige us to think that these infants necessarily die with original sin, so that there would be no way of salvation for them.

38. d) The Bull "*Auctorem fidei*" of Pope Pius VI is not a dogmatic definition of the existence of Limbo: the papal Bull confines itself to rejecting the Jansenist charge that the "Limbo" taught

---

[64] Cf. INNOCENT III, Letter to Humbert, Archbishop of Arles, *"Maiores Ecclesiae causas"*, *DS* 780.

[65] COUNCIL OF LYONS II, *Profession for Michael Paleologus, DS* 858; see above, footnote 48.

by scholastic theologians is identical with the "eternal life" promised to unbaptised infants by the ancient Pelagians. Pius VI did not condemn the Jansenists because they denied Limbo, but because they held that the defenders of Limbo were guilty of the heresy of Pelagius. By maintaining the freedom of the Catholic Schools to propose different solutions to the problem of the fate of unbaptised infants, the Holy See defended the common teaching as an acceptable and legitimate option, without endorsing it.

39. e) Pius XII's "Allocution to Italian Midwives",[66] which states that apart from Baptism "there is no other means of communicating [supernatural] life to the child who has not yet the use of reason", expressed the Church's faith regarding the necessity of grace to attain the beatific vision and the necessity of Baptism as the means to receive such grace.[67] The specification that little children (unlike adults) are unable to act on their own behalf, that is, are incapable of an act of reason and freedom that could "supply for Baptism", did not constitute a pronouncement on the content of current theological theories and did not prohibit the theological search for other ways of salvation. Pius XII rather recalled the limits within which the debate must take place and reasserted firmly the moral obligation to provide Baptism to infants in danger of death.

40. In summary: the affirmation that infants who die without Baptism suffer the privation of the beatific vision has long been the common doctrine of the Church, which must be distinguished from the faith of the Church. As for the theory that the privation of the beatific vision is their sole punishment, to the exclusion of any other pain, this is a theological opinion, despite its long acceptance in the West. The particular theological thesis concerning a "natural happiness" sometimes ascribed to these infants likewise constitutes a theological opinion.

41. Therefore, besides the theory of Limbo (which remains a possible theological opinion), there can be other ways to integrate and safeguard the principles of the faith grounded in Scripture: the

---

[66] *Acta Apostolicae Sedis* 43 (1951), 841.

[67] See above, 1.6 and below, 2.4.

creation of the human being in Christ and his vocation to communion with God; the universal salvific will of God; the transmission and the consequences of original sin; the necessity of grace in order to enter into the Kingdom of God and attain the vision of God; the uniqueness and universality of the saving mediation of Christ Jesus; and the necessity of Baptism for salvation. These other ways are not achieved by modifying the principles of the faith, or by elaborating hypothetical theories; rather, they seek an integration and coherent reconciliation of the principles of the faith under the guidance of the ecclesial magisterium, by giving more weight to God's universal salvific will and to solidarity in Christ (cf. *GS* 22) in order to account for the hope that infants dying without Baptism could enjoy eternal life in the beatific vision. In keeping with a methodological principle that what is less known must be investigated by way of what is better known, it appears that the point of departure for considering the destiny of these children should be the salvific will of God, the mediation of Christ and the gift of the Holy Spirit, and a consideration of the condition of children who receive Baptism and are saved through the action of the Church in the name of Christ. The destiny of unbaptised infants remains, however, a limit-case as regards theological inquiry: theologians should keep in mind the apophatic perspective of the Greek Fathers.

2. *Inquirere Vias Domini* Seeking to Discern God's Ways - Theological Principles

42. Since the theme under consideration concerns a topic for which no explicit answer is directly forthcoming from Revelation as embodied in Sacred Scripture and Tradition, the Catholic believer must have recourse to certain underlying theological principles which the Church, and specifically the magisterium, the guardian of the deposit of the faith, has articulated with the assistance of the Holy Spirit. As Vatican II affirms: "In Catholic doctrine there exists an order or "hierarchy" of truths since they vary in their relation to the foundation of the Christian faith" (*UR* 11). No human being can ultimately save him/herself. Salvation comes only from God the Father through Jesus Christ in the Holy Spirit. This fundamental truth (of the "absolute necessity" of God's saving act towards human beings) is unfolded in history through the mediation of the Church and its sacramental ministry. The *ordo tractandi* we will adopt here follows the *ordo salutis*, with one exception: we have put the anthropological dimension between the trinitarian and the ecclesiological-sacramental dimensions.

2.1. The Universal Salvific Will of God as Realized Through the Unique Mediation of Jesus Christ in the Holy Spirit

43. In the context of the discussion on the destiny of those infants who die without Baptism, the mystery of the universal salvific will of God is a fundamental and central principle. The depth of this mystery is reflected in the paradox of divine love which is manifested as both universal and preferential.

44. In the Old Testament, God is called the saviour of the nation of Israel (cf. *Ex* 6:6; *Dt* 7:8; 13:5; 32:15; 33:29; *Is* 41:14; 43:14; 44:24; *Ps* 78; 1 *M* 4:30). But his preferential love for Israel has a universal scope, which extends to individuals (cf. 2 *S* 22:18, 44, 49; *Ps* 25:5; 27:1), and all human beings: "Thou lovest all things that exist, and hast loathing for none of the things which thou hast made, for thou wouldst not have made anything if thou hast hated it" (*Ws* 11:24). Through Israel the gentile nations will find salvation

(cf. *Is* 2:1-4; 42:1; 60:1-14). "I will give you as a light to the nations, that my salvation may reach to the end of the earth" (*Is* 49:6).

45. This preferential and universal love of God is intertwined and realized in a unique and exemplary fashion in Jesus Christ, who is the unique Saviour of all (cf. *Ac* 4:12), but particularly of whoever becomes low or humble (*tapeinôsei*) like the "little ones". Indeed, as one who is gentle or humble in heart (cf. *Mt* 11:29), Jesus maintains a mysterious affinity and solidarity with them (cf. *Mt* 18:3-5; 10:40-42; 25:40,45). Jesus asserts that the care of these little ones is entrusted to the angels of God (cf. *Mt* 18:10). "So it is not the will of my Father who is in heaven that one of these little ones should perish" (*Mt* 18:14). This mystery of his will, according to the good pleasure of the Father,[68] is revealed through the Son[69] and dispensed by the gift of the Holy Spirit.[70]

46. The universality of the saving will of God the Father as realized through the unique and universal mediation of his Son, Jesus Christ, is forcefully expressed in the first letter to Timothy: "This is good, and it is acceptable in the sight of God our Saviour, who wills (*thelei*) all to be saved and to come to the knowledge of the truth. For there is one God, and there is one mediator between God and men, the man Christ Jesus, who gave himself as a ransom for all, the testimony to which was borne at the proper time" (1 *Tm* 2:3-6). The emphatic reiteration of "all" (vv. 1, 4, 6), and the justification of this universality on the basis of the uniqueness of God and of his mediator who himself is a man, suggests that nobody is excluded from this salvific will. Insofar as it is the object of prayer (cf. 1 *Tm* 2:1), this salvific will *(thelèma)* refers to a will which is sincere on the part of God, but, at times, is resisted by human beings.[71] Therefore we need to pray to Our Father in heaven that his will (*thelèma*) may be done on earth as it is in heaven (cf. *Mt* 6:10).

47. The mystery of this will, revealed to Paul as "the very least of all the saints" (*Ep* 3:8f.), has its roots in the Father's purpose to

---

[68] Cf. Ep 1:6, 9: "the purpose (*eudokía*) of his will".
[69] Cf. Lk 10:22: "the one to whom the Son chooses (*bouletai*) to reveal him".
[70] Cf. 1 Co 12:11: "who apportions to each one individually as he wills *(bouletai)*".
[71] Cf. for instance Mt 23:37.

make his only Son not just "the first-born among many brethren" (*Rm* 8:29), but also "the first-born of all creation ... [and] from the dead" (*Col* 1:15,18). This revelation allows one to discover in the mediation of the Son universal and cosmic dimensions, which overcome all divisions (cf. *GS* 13). With respect to the universality of humankind, the mediation of the Son surmounts (i) the various cultural, social and gender divisions: "there is neither Jew nor Greek... neither slave nor free... neither male nor female" (*Ga* 3:28); and (ii) the divisions caused by sin, internal (cf. *Rm* 7) as well as interpersonal (cf. *Ep* 2:14): "For as by one man's disobedience many were made sinners, so by one man's obedience many will be made righteous" (*Rm* 5:19). With respect to cosmic divisions, Paul explains that "For in him all the fulness of God was pleased to dwell, and through him to reconcile to himself all things, whether on earth or in heaven, by making peace by the blood of his cross" (*Col* 1:19-20). Both dimensions are brought together in the letter to the Ephesians (1:7-10): "In him we have redemption through his blood, the forgiveness of our trespasses...according to his purpose which he set forth in Christ...to unite all things in [Christ], things in heaven and things on earth".

48. Certainly we do not see yet the fulfilment of this mystery of salvation, "for in this hope we were saved" (*Rm* 8:24). The Holy Spirit indeed testifies that it is not yet realised, and at the same time encourages Christians to pray and to hope for the final resurrection: "We know that the whole creation has been groaning in travail together until now; and not only the creation, but we ourselves, who have the first fruits of the Spirit, groan inwardly while we wait for adoption as sons, the redemption of our bodies ... Likewise the Spirit helps us in our weakness; for we do not know how to pray as we ought, but the Spirit himself intercedes for us with sighs too deep for words" (*Rm* 8:22f., 26). So the groaning of the Spirit not only helps our prayers but encompasses so to speak the pains of all adults, of all children, of the whole of creation.[72]

[72] Cf. *CCC* 307.

49. The Synod of Quiercy (853) asserts: "Almighty God wishes all men without exception to be saved [1 *Tm* 2:4], although not all are saved. The fact that some are saved, however, is a gift of the Saviour, while the fact that others perish is the fault of those who perish".[73] Spelling out the positive implications of this statement as regards the universal solidarity of all in the mystery of Jesus Christ, the synod further asserts that: "As there is no man who was, is or will be, whose nature was not assumed in him [the Lord Jesus Christ], likewise there is no one who was, is or will be, for whom he did not suffer, even though not everyone [factually] is redeemed by his passion".[74]

50. This Christocentric conviction has found expression all through Catholic tradition. St Irenaeus, for instance, quotes the Pauline text asserting that Christ will return "to unite all things in him" (*Ep* 1:10) and that every knee should bow to him in heaven and on earth and under the earth and every tongue confess that Jesus Christ is Lord.[75] On his part, St Thomas Aquinas, once again basing himself on the Pauline text, has this to say: "Christ is the perfect mediator of God and men by reason of his having reconciled through his death the human race with God".[76]

51. The documents of Vatican II, not only quote the Pauline text in its entirety (cf. *LG* 60, *AG* 7), but also refer to it (cf. *LG* 49), and furthermore repeatedly use the designation *Unicus Mediator Christus* (*LG* 8, 14, 62). This core affirmation of Christological faith also finds expression in the post-conciliar papal magisterium: "And there is salvation in no one else, for there is no other name under heaven given among men by which we must be saved" (*Ac* 4:12). This statement...has a universal value, since for all people ... salvation can only come from Jesus Christ".[77]

52. The declaration *Dominus Iesus* succinctly sums up the Catholic conviction and attitude: "It must be firmly believed as a truth of Catholic faith that the universal salvific will of the one and triune

---

[73] *DS* 623.
[74] *DS* 624.
[75] See Irenaeus, *Adv.Haer.*, I, 10, 1 (PG 7, 550).
[76] Thomas Aquinas, *Summa Theologiae* III, q. 26, art. 1, *corpus*.
[77] John Paul II, Encyclical *Redemptoris Missio*, 5.

God is offered and accomplished once and for all in the mystery of the incarnation, death and resurrection of the Son of God".[78]

2.2. The Universality of Sin and the Universal Need of Salvation

53. The universal salvific will of God through Jesus Christ, in a mysterious relationship with the Church, is directed to all humans, who, according to the faith of the Church, are sinners in need of salvation. Already in the Old Testament, the all-pervading nature of human sin is mentioned in almost every book. The book of Genesis affirms that sin did not find its origin with God but with human beings, because God created everything and saw that it was good (cf. *Gn* 1:31). From the moment the human race began to increase on the earth, God had to reckon with the sinfulness of humankind: "The Lord saw that the wickedness of man was great in the earth, and that every imagination of the thoughts of his heart was only evil continually". He was even "sorry that he had made man on the earth", and ordered a flood to destroy every living thing, except Noah who found favour in his eyes (cf. *Gn* 6:5-7). But even the flood did not change the human inclination to sin: "I will never again curse the ground because of man, for the imagination of man's heart is evil from his youth" (*Gn* 8:21). The Old Testament writers are convinced that sin is deeply rooted and pervasive in humanity (cf. *Pr* 20:9; *Qo* 7:20.29). Hence the frequent petitions for God's indulgence, as in Psalm 143:2: "Enter not into judgment with thy servant; for no man living is righteous before thee", or in the prayer of Solomon: "If they sin against thee - for there is no man who does not sin - ...if they repent with all their mind and with all their heart...then hear thou in heaven thy dwelling place their prayer...and forgive thy people who have sinned against thee" (1 *K* 8:46ff.). There are some texts which speak of the sinfulness from birth. The psalmist affirms: "Behold, I was brought forth in iniquity, and in sin did my mother conceive me" (*Ps* 51:7). And the statement of Eliphaz: "What is man, that he can be clean? Or he that is born of a woman, that he can be righteous?" (*Jb* 15:14; cf. 25:4), is in agreement with Job's own convictions (cf. *Jb* 14:1.4) and those of other biblical writers (cf. *Ps* 58:3; *Is* 48:8). In Wisdom

[78] Congregation for the Doctrine of the Faith, Declaration *Dominus Iesus*, 14.

Literature there is even a beginning of reflection on the effects of the sin of the ancestors, Adam and Eve, on the whole of humankind: "But through the devil's envy death entered the world, and those who belong to his party experience it" (*Ws* 2:24); "From a woman sin had its beginning, and because of her we all die" (*Si* 25:24).[79]

54. For Paul, the universality of the redemption brought by Jesus Christ finds its counterpart in the universality of sin. When Paul in his letter to the Romans asserts "that all, both Jews and Gentiles, are under the power of sin" (*Rm* 3:9)[80] and that no one can be excluded from this universal verdict, he naturally bases this on Scripture: "As it is written: 'None is righteous, no, not one; no one understands, no one seeks for God. All have turned aside, together they have gone wrong; no one does good, not even one'" (*Rm* 3:10-12, quoting *Qo* 7:20 and *Ps* 14:1-3 which is identical to *Ps* 53:1-3). On the one side, all human beings are sinners and need to be delivered through the redemptive death and resurrection of Jesus Christ, the new Adam. Not the works of the Law, but only faith in Jesus Christ can save humanity, Jews and Gentiles alike. On the other side, the sinful condition of humankind is linked to the sin of the first man, Adam. This solidarity with the first man, Adam, is expressed in two Pauline texts: 1 Co 15:21 and especially Rm 5:12: "Therefore as sin came into the world through one man and death through sin, and so death spread to all men because [Gr. *eph'hō*: other possible translations 'on the basis of which' or 'with the result that'][81] all men sinned..." In this anacolouth, the primary causality for the sinful and mortal condition of humankind

---

[79] Other attestations of the Jewish belief about Adam's influence in the time of Paul are: 2 Apoc. Bar. 17:3; 23:4; 48:42; 54:15; 4 Ezra 3:7; 7:118; "O Adam, what have you done? Though it was you who sinned, the fall was not yours alone, but ours too who are your descendants".

[80] Cf. Rm 3:23: "All have sinned and fall short of the glory of God".

[81] In the Western Church, the Greek phrase *eph'hō* was understood as a relative clause with a masculine pronoun referring to Adam or a neuter pronoun referring to Sin (*peccatum*) (cf. Vetus Latina and Vulgate *in quo*). Augustine at first accepted both interpretations, but when he realized that the Greek word for sin was feminine (*hamartia*) he opted for the first interpretation, which would imply the notion of incorporation of all human beings in Adam. He was followed by many Latin theologians, either "sive in Adamo, sive in peccato", or "in Adamo". The latter interpretation was not known in the Eastern Church before John Damascene. Several Greek Fathers understood *eph'hō* as "because of whom", i.e. Adam, "all sinned". The phrase *eph'hō* has also been understood as a conjunction and translated as "since, because", "on condition that", or "with the result that, so that". J. FITZMYER (*Romans* [AB, 33], New York, 1992, 413-416) discusses eleven different interpretations and opts for the latter possibility of a consecutive meaning: "*Eph'hō*, then, would mean that Paul is expressing a result, the sequel to Adam's baleful influence on humanity by the ratification of his sin in the sins of all individuals" (p. 416).

is ascribed to Adam, no matter how one understands the phrase *eph' hō*. The universal causality of Adam's sin is presupposed in Rm 5:15a, 16a, 17a, 18a and clearly expressed in 5:19a: "by one man's disobedience many were made sinners". However, Paul never explains how Adam's sin is transmitted. Against Pelagius, who thought that Adam influenced humanity by giving it a bad example, Augustine objected that Adam's sin was transmitted by propagation or heredity, and so brought the doctrine of "original sin" to its classical expression.[82] Under Augustine's influence, the Western Church almost unanimously interpreted Rm 5:12 in the sense of hereditary "sin".[83]

55. Following this, the Council of Trent in its Fifth Session (1546), defined: "If anyone asserts that Adam's sin harmed only him and not his descendants and that the holiness and justice received from God which he lost was lost only for him and not for us also; or that, stained by the sin of disobedience, he transmitted to all humankind only death and the sufferings of the body but not sin as well which is the death of the soul, *anathema sit*. For, he contradicts the words of the apostle: "Sin came into the world through one man and death through sin, and so [death] spread to all as all men sinned in him" [*Rm* 5:12 *Vulg*.].[84]

56. As the *Catechism of the Catholic Church* puts it: "The doctrine of original sin is, so to speak, the 'reverse side' of the Good News that Jesus is the saviour of all men, that all need salvation and that salvation is offered to all through Christ. The Church, which has the mind of Christ, knows very well that we cannot tamper with the revelation of original sin without undermining the mystery of Christ".[85]

---

[82] *De nuptiis et concupiscentia* II,12,15 (PL, 44, 450): *"Non ego finxi originale peccatum quod catholica fides credit antiquitus"*.

[83] The *Catechism of the Catholic Church* 404 speaks of "a sin which will be transmitted by propagation to all mankind, that is, by the transmission of a human nature deprived of original holiness and justice". And it adds: "And that is why original sin is called 'sin' only in an analogical sense: it is a sin 'contracted' and not 'committed' – a state and not an act".

[84] COUNCIL OF TRENT, Fifth Session, Decree on Original Sin, *DS* 1512; *ND* 509. The decree of Trent echoes the second canon of the Second Council of Orange (529).

[85] *CCC* 389.

2.3. The Need for the Church

57. Catholic tradition has constantly affirmed that the Church is necessary for salvation as the historical mediation of the redemptive work of Jesus Christ. This conviction found its classical expression in the adage of St Cyprian: "*Salus extra Ecclesiam non est*".[86] The Second Vatican Council has reiterated this faith conviction: "Basing itself on Scripture and tradition, it [the Council] teaches that the Church, a pilgrim now on earth, is necessary for salvation: the one Christ is mediator and the way of salvation; he is present to us in his body which is the Church. He himself explicitly asserted the necessity of faith and Baptism (cf. *Mk* 16:16; *Jn* 3:5), and thereby affirmed at the same time the necessity of the Church which men enter through Baptism as through a door. Hence they could not be saved who, knowing that the Catholic Church was founded as necessary by God through Christ, would refuse either to enter it, or to remain in it" (*LG* 14). The Council expounded the mystery of the Church at length: "The Church, in Christ, is in the nature of [a] sacrament - a sign and instrument, that is, of communion with God and of the unity among all men" (*LG* 1); "Just as Christ carried out the work of redemption in poverty and oppression, so the Church is called to follow the same path if she is to communicate the fruits of salvation to men" (*LG* 8). "Rising from the dead (cf. *Rm* 6:9) he [Christ] sent his life-giving Spirit upon his disciples and through him set up his Body which is the Church as the universal sacrament of salvation" (*LG* 48). What is striking in these quotations is the universal extent of the Church's mediating role in ministering God's salvation: "the unity among *all men*", "salvation of [all] *men*", "*universal* sacrament of salvation".

58. In the face of new problems and situations and of an exclusive interpretation of the adage: "*salus extra ecclesiam*

---

[86] Cyprian, *Epistola ad Iubaianum* 73, 21 (PL 3, 1123); see also Council of Florence, Bull "Cantate Domino", *DS* 1351; *ND* 810: "The holy Roman Church [...] firmly believes, professes and preaches that 'no one remaining outside the Catholic Church, not only pagans', but also Jews, heretics or schismatics, can become partakers of eternal life; but they will go to the 'eternal fire prepared for the devil and his angels' [Mt 25:41], unless before the end of their life they are joined to (*aggregati*) it ... 'And no one can be saved, no matter how much alms one has given, even if shedding one's blood for the name of Christ, unless one remains in the bosom and unity of the Catholic Church.'" (FULGENTIUS of RUSPE, *Liber De fide ad Petrum, liber unus*, 38, 79 and 39, 80).

non est",[87] the magisterium, in recent times, has articulated a more nuanced understanding as to the manner in which a saving relationship with the Church can be realized. The Allocution of Pope Pius IX, *Singulari Quadam* (1854) clearly states the issues involved: "It must, of course, be held as a matter of faith that outside the apostolic Roman Church no one can be saved, that the Church is the only ark of salvation, and that whoever does not enter it, will perish in the flood. On the other hand, it must likewise be held as certain that those who live in ignorance of the true religion, if such ignorance be invincible, are not subject to any guilt in this matter before the eyes of the Lord".[88]

59. The *Letter of the Holy Office to the Archbishop of Boston* (1949) offers further specifications. "To gain eternal salvation, it is not always required that a person be incorporated in reality (*reapse*) as a member of the Church, but it is necessary that one belong to it at least in desire and longing (*voto et desiderio*). It is not always necessary that this desire be explicit as it is with catechumens. When one is invincibly ignorant, God also accepts an implicit desire, so called because it is contained in the good disposition of soul by which a person wants his or her will to be conformed to God's will".[89]

60. The universal salvific will of God, realized through Jesus Christ, in the Holy Spirit, which includes the Church as the universal sacrament of salvation, finds expression in Vatican II: "All men are called to this Catholic unity which prefigures and promotes universal peace. And in different ways to it belong, or are related: all the Catholic faithful, others who believe in Christ and finally all mankind called by God's grace to salvation" (*LG* 13). That the unique and universal mediation of Jesus Christ is realized in the context of a relationship with the Church is further reiterated by the post-Conciliar papal magisterium. Speaking of those who have not had the opportunity to come to know or accept Gospel revelation – even in their case, the encyclical *Redemptoris Missio* has this to

---

[87] Cf. BONIFACE VIII, Bull *"Unam Sanctam"*: *"Porro subesse Romano Pontifici omni humanae creaturae declaramus, dicimus, diffinimus omnino esse de necessitate salutis"*, *DS* 875; cp. *DS* 1351; *ND* 875: "Furthermore we declare, state and define that it is absolutely necessary for the salvation of all human beings that they submit to the Roman Pontiff".

[88] Pius IX, Allocution *"Singulari Quadam"*, DS 2865i; *ND* 813.

[89] Letter of the Holy Office to the Archbishop of Boston, *DS* 3870; *ND* 855.

say: "Salvation in Christ is accessible by virtue of a grace ... which has a mysterious relationship to the Church".[90]

2.4. The Necessity of Sacramental Baptism

61. God the Father intends to configure all human beings to Christ by the Holy Spirit, who transforms and empowers them by his grace. Ordinarily, this configuration to Jesus Christ takes place through sacramental Baptism, whereby one is conformed to Christ, receives the Holy Spirit, is liberated from sin and becomes a member of the Church.

62. The numerous baptismal statements in the New Testament, in their variety, articulate the different dimensions of the significance of Baptism as understood by the early Christian community. In the first place, Baptism is designated as the forgiveness of sins, as cleansing (cf. *Ep* 5:26), or as a sprinkling which cleanses the heart from an evil conscience (cf. *Heb* 10:22; 1 *P* 3:21). "Repent, and be baptised every one of you in the name of Jesus Christ for the forgiveness of your sins; and you shall receive the gift of the Holy Spirit" (*Ac* 2:38; cf. *Ac* 22:16). The baptised are thus configured to Jesus Christ: "We were buried therefore with him by baptism into death, so that as Christ was raised from the dead by the glory of the Father, we too might walk in newness of life" (*Rm* 6:4).

63. Furthermore, the activity of the Holy Spirit in connection with Baptism is repeatedly referred to (cf. *Tt* 3:5). It is the belief of the Church that the Holy Spirit is imparted with Baptism (cf. 1 *Co* 6:11; *Tt* 3:5). The Risen Christ is active through his Spirit, who makes us children of God (cf. *Rm* 8:14), confident to call God Father (cf. *Ga* 4:6).

64. Finally, there are the statements about being "added" to the People of God in the context of Baptism, of being baptised "into one body" (*Ac* 2:41). Baptism results in the incorporation of the human person into the People of God, the Body of Christ and the spiritual temple. Paul speaks of "being baptised into one body" (1 *Co* 12:13). Luke, instead, of "being added" to the Church through

[90] JOHN PAUL II, Encyclical *Redemptoris Missio*, 10.

Baptism (*Ac* 2:41). Through Baptism, the believer is not only an individual, but becomes a member of the People of God. He or she becomes a member of the Church which Peter calls "a chosen race, a royal priesthood, a holy nation, God's own people" (1 *P* 2:9).

65. The tradition of conferring sacramental Baptism is extended to all, even to infants. Among the New Testament testimonies of Christian Baptism in the book of the Acts of the Apostles, there are instances of "household baptisms" (cf. *Ac* 16:15; 16:33; 18:8), which possibly included children. The ancient praxis of baptizing children,[91] endorsed by the Fathers and the magisterium of the Church, is accepted as an essential part of the faith understanding of the Catholic Church. The Council of Trent will affirm: "In accordance with apostolic tradition, even children who of themselves cannot have yet committed any sin are truly baptized for the remission of sins, so that by regeneration they may be cleansed from what they contracted through generation. For "unless one is born of water and the Spirit, one cannot enter the Kingdom of God [*Jn* 3:5]".[92]

66. The necessity of the sacrament of Baptism is proclaimed and professed as integral to the Christian faith understanding. On the basis of the command as found in Mt 28:19ff. and Mk 16:15, and of the prescription laid down in Jn 3:5,[93] the Christian community has from the earliest time, believed in the necessity of Baptism for salvation. While considering sacramental Baptism necessary inasmuch as it is the ordinary way established by Jesus Christ to

---

[91] Polycarp may be an indirect witness to this, since he declares before the proconsul: "For 86 years I have been serving Him [the Christ]", *Martyrium Polycarpi* 9,3. Polycarp's martyrdom probably occurred during the final years of the reign of Antoninus Pius (156-160).

[92] COUNCIL OF TRENT, Fifth Session, Decree on Original Sin, *DS* 1514; *ND* 511. The canon echoes the second canon of the Council of Carthage (418), *DS* 23.

[93] Taking into account the Old Testament texts regarding the outpouring of the Spirit by God, the principal idea in Jn 3:5 seems to refer to God's gift of the Spirit. If natural life is attributable to the fact of God giving the spirit to human beings, analogously eternal life begins when God gives his Holy Spirit to human beings. Cf. R.E. BROWN, *The Gospel according to John (1 – XII)*, The Anchor Bible, vol. 29, Doubleday and Co: New York, 1966, 140. In this regard, Brown observes: "The baptismal motif that is woven into the text of the whole scene is secondary; the phrase 'of water' in which the baptismal motif expresses itself most clearly may have been always part of the scene, although originally not having a specific reference to Christian Baptism; or the phase may have been added to the tradition later in order to bring out the baptismal motif". (*Ibid*., 143). The Lord stresses the necessity of a birth "of water and spirit" to enter into the kingdom of God. In Christian Tradition, this has been understood as pointing to the "sacrament of Baptism", although the "sacramental" reading is a limitation of the pneumatological meaning. Read in this way, the issue can be raised as to whether the text expresses here a general principle without exception. One should be aware of the slight shift in interpretation.

configure human beings to himself, the Church has never taught the "absolute necessity" of sacramental Baptism for salvation; there are other avenues whereby the configuration with Christ can be realized. Already in the early Christian community, it was accepted that martyrdom, the "Baptism of blood", was a substitute for sacramental Baptism. Furthermore, there was the acknowledgement of the Baptism of desire. In this regard, the words of Thomas Aquinas are pertinent: "The sacrament of Baptism may be wanting to someone in two ways. First, both in reality and in desire; as is the case with those who neither are baptised, nor wish to be baptised... Secondly, the sacrament of Baptism may be wanting to anyone in reality but not in desire...Such a man can obtain salvation without being actually baptised on account of his desire for Baptism".[94] The Council of Trent acknowledges "Baptism of desire" as a way whereby one can be justified without the actual reception of the sacrament of Baptism: "After the promulgation of the Gospel, this transition [from sin to justice] cannot take place without the bath of regeneration or the desire for it for as it is written: 'Unless one is born of water and the Spirit, one cannot enter the kingdom of God (*Jn* 3:5)'".[95]

67. The Christian faith affirmation of the necessity of sacramental Baptism for salvation cannot be depleted of its existential significance by being reduced to a merely theoretical affirmation. On the other hand, God's freedom over the saving means given by him must be equally respected. Consequently, one must avoid any attempt to oppose sacramental Baptism, the Baptism of desire and Baptism of blood as antithetical. They are but expressions of the creative polarities within the realization of God's universal salvific will on behalf of humanity, which include both a real possibility of salvation, and a salvific dialogue in freedom with the human person. It is precisely this dynamism which impels the Church, as the universal sacrament of salvation, to summon everyone to repentance, to faith and to sacramental Baptism. This dialogue in grace is elicited only when the human person is existentially capable of a response in the concrete – which is not the case with infants. Hence the need for parents and godparents to speak on behalf of infants who are baptized. But what of infants who die without Baptism?

---

[94] Thomas Aquinas, *Summa Theologiae* III, q. 68, art. 2, *corpus*.

[95] COUNCIL OF TRENT, Sixth Session, Decree on Justification, *DS* 1524; *ND* 1928.

2.5. Hope and Prayer for Universal Salvation

68. Christians are people of hope. They have set their hope "on the living God, who is the saviour of all, especially of those who believe" (1 *Tm* 4:10). They ardently desire that all human beings, unbaptised children included, may share in God's glory and live with Christ (cf. 1 *Th* 5:9-11; *Rm* 8:2-5; 23-35), in keeping with the recommendation of Theophylactus: "If he [our God] wants all men to be saved, you should also want it, and imitate God".[96] This Christian hope is a "hope ... against hope" (*Rm* 4:18), going far beyond any form of human hope. It takes its example from Abraham, our father in faith. Abraham put great trust in the promises that God had given him. He trusted ("hoped") in God against all human evidence or odds ("against hope"). So Christians, even when they do not see how unbaptised children can be saved, nevertheless dare to hope that God will embrace them in his saving mercy. They are also prepared to make a defence to any one who calls them to account for the hope that is in them (cf. 1 *P* 3:15). When they meet mothers and parents in distress because their children died before or after birth, without being baptised, they feel urged to explain to them why their own hope for salvation can also extend to those infants or children.[97]

69. Christians are people of prayer. They take to heart the admonition of Paul: "First of all, then, I urge that supplications, prayers, intercessions, and thanksgivings be made for all" (1 *Tm* 2:1). This universal prayer is acceptable to God who "desires all men to be saved and to come to the knowledge of truth" (1 *Tm* 2:4), and to whose creative power "nothing is impossible" (*Jb* 42:2; *Mk* 10:27; 12:24-27; *Lk* 1:37). It is based on the hope that the whole creation will finally share in the glory of God (cf. *Rm* 8:22-27). Such a prayer is in line with St John Chrysostom's admonition: "Imitate God. If he wants all to be saved, then it is reasonable that one should pray for all".[98]

---

[96] Theophylactus, *In 1 Tm 2,4* (PG 125, 32): *Ei pantas anthrôpous thelè sôthènai ekeinos, thele kai su, kai mimou ton theon.*

[97] It is notable that the *editio typica* of the encyclical of Pope John Paul II, *Evangelium Vitae*, has replaced paragraph 99 which read: "You will come to understand that nothing is definitively lost and you will also be able to ask forgiveness from your child, who is now living in the Lord" (a phrasing which was susceptible to a faulty interpretation), by this definitive text: *"Infantem autem vestrum potestis Eidem Patri Eiusque misericordiae cum spe committere"* (cf. *AAS* 87 (1995), 515), which may be translated as follows: "You can entrust your child to the same Father and to his mercy with hope".

[98] John Chrysostom, *In 1 Tm. homil.* 7,2 (PG 62, 536): *Mimou Theon. Ei pantas anthrôpous thelei sôthènai, eikotôs huper hapantôn dei euchesthai.*

3. *Spes Orans*
Reasons for Hope

3.1. The New Context

70. The two preceding chapters, considering the history of Christian reflection on the destiny of unbaptised infants[99] and the theological principles that bear upon this issue,[100] respectively, have presented a chiaroscuro. On the one hand, in many ways, the underpinning Christian theological principles seem to favour the salvation of unbaptised infants in accordance with God's universal salvific will. On the other hand, however, it cannot be denied that there has been a rather longstanding doctrinal tradition (whose theological value is doubtless not definitive), which, in its concern to safeguard and not compromise other truths of the Christian theological edifice, has expressed either a certain reticence in this regard, or even a clear refusal to envisage the salvation of these infants. There is a fundamental continuity in the Church's reflection upon the mystery of salvation from generation to generation under the guidance of the Holy Spirit. Within that mystery, the question of the eternal destiny of infants who die unbaptised is "one of the most difficult to solve in the structure of theology".[101] It is a "limit-case" where vital tenets of faith, especially the need of Baptism for salvation and the universal salvific will of God, can easily appear to be in tension. With respect for the wisdom and fidelity of those who have investigated this difficult matter before, but also with a keen awareness that the magisterium of the Church has specifically and perhaps providentially opted, at key moments in the history of doctrine,[102] not to define that these infants are deprived of the beatific vision but to keep the question open, we have considered how the Spirit may be guiding the Church at this point in history to reflect anew on this exceptionally delicate issue (cf. *DV* 8).

---

[99] See above, Chapter 1.

[100] See above, Chapter 2.

[101] Congar, *Vaste monde ma paroisse: Vérité et dimensions du Salut*, Paris: Témoignage Chrétien, 1968, 169: *"un de ceux dont la solution est la plus difficile ensynthèse théologique"*.

[102] See above, Chapter 1.5 & 1.6.

71. The Second Vatican Council called the Church to read the signs of the times and to interpret them in the light of the Gospel (cf. *GS* 4, 11), "in order that the revealed truth may be more deeply penetrated, better understood, and more suitably presented" (*GS* 44). In other words, engagement with the world for which Christ suffered, died and rose again, is always for the Church, which is the body of Christ, an occasion to deepen her understanding of the Lord himself and of his love, and indeed of herself, an occasion to penetrate more deeply the message of salvation entrusted to her. It is possible to identify various signs of our modern times that prompt a renewed awareness of aspects of the Gospel which particularly bear upon the question under consideration. In some ways, they provide a new context for its consideration at the start of the 21st century.

72. a) The warfare and turmoil of the 20th century, and the yearning of humanity for peace and unity, shown by the founding of, e.g., the United Nations Organization, the European Union, the African Union, have helped the Church to understand more deeply the importance of the theme of communion in the Gospel message and so to develop an ecclesiology of communion (cf. *LG* 4, 9; *UR* 2; *GS* 12, 24).

73. b) Many people today grapple with the temptation to despair. The crisis of hope in the contemporary world leads the Church to a deeper appreciation of the hope that is central to the Christian Gospel. "There is one body and one Spirit, just as you were called to the one hope that belongs to your call" (*Ep* 4:4). Christians are particularly called today to be witnesses to hope and ministers of hope in the world (cf. *LG* 48, 49; *GS* 1). The Church in its universality and catholicity is the bearer of a hope that extends to all humankind, and Christians have a mission to offer that hope to everyone.

74. c) The development of global communications, graphically highlighting all the suffering in the world, has been an occasion for the Church to understand God's love, mercy and compassion more profoundly, and to appreciate the primacy of charity. God is merciful, and, faced with the enormity of the world's pain,

we learn to trust and glorify God "who by the power at work within us is able to do far more abundantly than all that we ask or think" (*Ep* 3:20).

75. d) People everywhere are scandalised by the suffering of children and want to enable children to achieve their potential.[103] In such a setting, the Church naturally recalls and ponders anew various New Testament texts expressing the preferential love of Jesus: "Let the children come to me...for to such belongs the kingdom of heaven" (*Mt* 19:14; cf. *Lk* 18:15-16, 'infants'); "Whoever receives one such in my name receives me" (*Mk* 9:37); "unless you turn and become like children, you will never enter the kingdom of heaven" (*Mt* 18:3); "Whoever humbles himself like this child, he is the greatest in the kingdom of heaven" (*Mt* 18:4); "whoever causes one of these little ones who believe in me to sin, it would be better for him to have a great millstone fastened around his neck and to be drowned in the depth of the sea" (*Mt* 18:6); "See that you do not despise one of these little ones; for I tell you that in heaven their angels always behold the face of my Father who is in heaven" (*Mt* 18:10). So the Church renews her commitment to show Christ's own love and care for children (cf. *LG* 11; *GS* 48, 50).

76. e) Increased travel and contact among people of different faiths and the great increase of dialogue between people of different religions have encouraged the Church to develop a greater awareness of the manifold and mysterious ways of God (cf. *NA* 1, 2), and of her own mission in this context.

77. The development of an ecclesiology of communion, a theology of hope, an appreciation of divine mercy, together with a renewed concern for the welfare of infants and an ever-increasing awareness that the Holy Spirit works in the lives of all "in a way known to God" (*GS* 22), all of these features of our modern age constitute a new context for the examination of our question. This may be a providential moment for its reconsideration. By the grace of the Holy Spirit, the Church in its engagement with the world of our time has gained deeper insights into God's revelation that can cast new light on our question.

---

[103] Events such as Live Aid, 1985, and Live 8, 2005.

78. Hope is the all-embracing context of our reflections and report. The Church of today responds to the signs of our own times with renewed hope for the world at large and, with particular regard to our question, for unbaptised infants who die.[104] We must here and now give an account of that hope (cf. 1 *P* 3:15). In the last fifty years or so, the magisterium of the Church has shown an increasing openness to the possibility of the salvation of unbaptised infants, and the *sensus fidelium* seems to have been developing in the same direction. Christians constantly experience, most powerfully in the liturgy, Christ's victory over sin and death,[105] God's infinite mercy, and the loving communion of the saints in heaven, all of which increases our hope. There the hope that is in us, that we must proclaim and explain, is regularly renewed, and it is from that experience of hope that various considerations can now be offered.

79. It must be clearly acknowledged that the Church does not have sure knowledge about the salvation of unbaptised infants who die. She knows and celebrates the glory of the Holy Innocents, but the destiny of the generality of infants who die without Baptism has not been revealed to us, and the Church teaches and judges only with regard to what has been revealed. What we do positively know of God, Christ and the Church gives us grounds to hope for their salvation, as must now be explained.

3.2. God's Merciful Philanthropia

80. God is rich in mercy, *dives in misericordia* (*Ep* 2:4). The Byzantine liturgy frequently praises God's philanthropy; God is the "lover of man".[106] Moreover, God's loving purpose, now revealed through the Spirit, is beyond our imagining: "what God has prepared for those who love him" is something "no eye has seen, nor ear heard, nor the heart of man conceived" (1 *Co* 2:9-10, quoting *Is* 64:4). Those who grieve over the fate of infants who die unbaptised, especially their parents, are often themselves

[104] *CCC* 1261.

[105] Christ is risen from the dead. By death He conquered death, and to those in the grave he granted life" (Easter troparion of the Byzantine liturgy). This paschal verse is sung many times on each of the forty days of the Easter season in the Byzantine tradition. It is, thus, the principal Easter hymn.

[106] In all its ceremonies and celebrations, the Byzantine liturgy praises God's merciful love: "For You are a merciful God who loves mankind, and we glorify You, Father, Son, and Holy Spirit, now and ever and forever".

people who love God, people whom these words should console. In particular, the following observations can be made:

81. a) God's grace reaches all people and his providence embraces all. The Second Vatican Council teaches that God does not deny "the assistance necessary for salvation" to those who, without any fault of their own, have not yet arrived at an explicit knowledge of God, but who, with the help of grace, "strive to lead a good life". God enlightens all people "that they may at length have life" (cf. *LG* 16). Again it teaches that grace is "active invisibly" in the hearts of all people of good will (*GS* 22). These words apply directly to those above the age of reason, who are making responsible decisions, but it is difficult to deny their applicability also to those below the age of reason. The following words, in particular, seem truly universal in their scope. "For since Christ died for all, and since all are in fact called to one and the same destiny, which is divine [*cumque vocatio hominis ultima revera una sit, scilicet divina*], we must hold that the Holy Spirit offers to all the possibility of being made partners, in a way known to God, in the paschal mystery" (*GS* 22). This profound sentence of Vatican II takes us into the heart of the loving purpose of the blessed Trinity and stresses that God's purpose exceeds our understanding.

82. b) God does not demand the impossible of us.[107] Furthermore, God's power is not restricted to the sacraments: 'Deus virtutem suam non alligavit sacramentis quin possit sine sacramentis effectum sacramentorum conferre' (God did not bind His power to the sacraments, so as to be unable to bestow the sacramental effect without conferring the sacrament).[108] God can therefore give the grace of Baptism without the sacrament being conferred, and this fact should particularly be recalled when the conferring of Baptism would be impossible. The need for the sacrament is not absolute. What is absolute is humanity's need for the *Ursakrament* which is Christ himself. All salvation comes from him and therefore, in some way, through the Church.[109]

---

[107] AUGUSTINE, *De natura et gratia* 43, 50 (PL 44, 271).

[108] AQUINAS, *Summa Theologiae* III, 64, 7; cf. III, 64, 3; III, 66, 6; III, 68, 2.

[109] Below, 3.4. & 3.5.

83. c) At all times and in all circumstances, God provides a remedy of salvation for humanity.[110] This was the teaching of Aquinas,[111] and already before him of Augustine[112] and Leo the Great.[113] It is also found in Cajetan.[114] Pope Innocent III specifically focused on the situation of children: "Far from us the thought that all the small children, of whom such a great multitude dies every day, should perish without the merciful God, who wishes no one to perish, having provided for them also some means of salvation ... We say that two kinds of sin must be distinguished, original and actual: original which is contracted without consent and actual which is committed with consent. Thus original sin, which is contracted without consent is remitted without consent by the power of the sacrament [of Baptism]; ...".[115] Innocent was defending infant Baptism as the means provided by God for the salvation of the many infants who die each day. We may ask, however, on the basis of a more searching application of the same principle, whether God also provides some remedy for those infants who die without Baptism. There is no question of denying Innocent's teaching that those who die in original sin are deprived of the beatific vision.[116] What we may ask and are asking is whether infants who die without Baptism necessarily die in original sin, without a divine remedy.

---

[110] Thomas Aquinas, *In IV Sent.* Dist.1, q. 2, a. 4, q.1, a. 2: *"in quolibet statu post peccatum fuit aliquod remedium per quod originale peccatum ex virtute passionis Christi tolleretur"*.

[111] See also note 109, above.

[112] AUGUSTINE, *Ep.* 102, 2, 12.

[113] LEO THE GREAT, *In nat. Domini* 4,1 (PL 54, 203): *"Sacramentum salutis humanae nulla umquam antiquitate cessavit... Semper quidem, dilectissimi, diversis modis multisque mensuris humano generi bonitas divina consuluit. Et plurima providentiae suae munera omnibus retro saeculis clementer impertuit"*.

[114] CAJETAN, *In IIIam Part.*, q. 68, a.11: *"Rationabile esse ut divina misericordia provideret homini in quocumque naturali statu de aliquo remedio salutis"* (It is reasonable that God's mercy should provide man, in whatever natural state [he be], with some remedy of salvation). Cajetan was actually looking to the time before Christ when there was a kind of *sacramentum naturae*, e.g. offering a sacrifice, which was the occasion (but not the cause) of grace. He understood the situation of human beings prior to Christ to be "in the time of the law of nature" and understood the situation of unbaptised infants similarly. He therefore applied his principle in favour of the idea of Limbo as the destiny of such infants. His fundamental point, however, is very important and does not necessarily lead to the conclusion of Limbo: namely, that at all times in history and in all circumstances God cares for the human situation and offers appropriate opportunities for salvation.

[115] INNOCENT III, Letter to Humbert, Archbishop of Arles, *ND*, 1409, 506; *DS*, 780 *"Absit enim, ut universi parvuli pereant, quorum quotidie tanta multitudo moritur, quin et ipse misericors Deus, qui neminem vult perire, aliquod remedium procuraverit ad salutem... Dicimus distinguendum, quod peccatum est duplex: originale scilicet et actuale: originale, quod absque consensu contrahitur, et actuale, quod committitur cum consensu. Originale igitur, quod sine consensu contrahitur, sine consensu per vim remittitur sacramenti; ..."*

[116] *DS* 780.

84. With confidence that in all circumstances God provides, how might we imagine such a remedy? The following are ways by which unbaptised infants who die may perhaps be united to Christ.

85. a) Broadly, we may discern in those infants who themselves suffer and die a saving conformity to Christ in his own death, and a companionship with him. Christ himself on the Cross bore the weight of all of humanity's sin and death, and all suffering and death thereafter is an engagement with his own enemy (cf. 1 *Co* 15:26), a participation in his own battle, in the midst of which we can find him alongside us (cf. *Dn* 3:24-25 [91-92]; *Rm* 8:31-39; 2 *Tm* 4:17). His Resurrection is the source of humanity's hope (cf.1 *Co* 15:20); in him alone is there life in abundance (cf. *Jn* 10:10); and the Holy Spirit offers to all a participation in his paschal mystery (cf. *GS* 22).

86. b) Some of the infants who suffer and die do so as victims of violence. In their case, we may readily refer to the example of the Holy Innocents and discern an analogy in the case of these infants to the baptism of blood which brings salvation. Albeit unknowingly, the Holy Innocents suffered and died on account of Christ; their murderers were seeking to kill the infant Jesus. Just as those who took the lives of the Holy Innocents were motivated by fear and selfishness, so the lives particularly of unborn babies today are often endangered by the fear or selfishness of others. In that sense, they are in solidarity with the Holy Innocents. Moreover, they are in solidarity with the Christ who said: "Truly, I say to you, as you did it to one of the least of these my brethren, you did it to me" (*Mt* 25:40). How vital it is for the Church to proclaim the hope and generosity that are intrinsic to the Gospel and essential for the protection of life.

87. c) It is also possible that God simply acts to give the gift of salvation to unbaptised infants by analogy with the gift of salvation given sacramentally to baptized infants.[117] We may perhaps compare this to God's unmerited gift to Mary at her Immaculate

[117] The situation of unbaptised infants may be considered by analogy with that of baptised infants, as here. More problematically, it may also perhaps be considered by analogy with the situation of unbaptised adults, see below, footnote 127.

Conception, by which he simply acted to give her in advance the grace of salvation in Christ.

3.3. Solidarity with Christ

88. There is a fundamental unity and solidarity between Christ and the whole human race. By his Incarnation, the Son of God has united himself, in some way ("*quodammodo*"), with every human being (*GS* 22).[118] There is, therefore, no one who is untouched by the mystery of the Word made flesh. Humanity, and indeed all creation, has been objectively changed by the very fact of the Incarnation and objectively saved by the suffering, death and resurrection of Christ.[119] However, that objective salvation must be subjectively appropriated (cf. *Ac* 2:37-38; 3:19), ordinarily by the personal exercise of free will in favour of grace in adults, with or without sacramental Baptism, or by infants' reception of sacramental Baptism. The situation of unbaptised infants is problematic precisely because of their presumed lack of free will.[120] Their situation acutely raises the question of the relationship between the objective salvation won by Christ and original sin, and the question also of the exact import of the Conciliar word, "*quodammodo*".

89. Christ lived, died and rose again for all. Pauline teaching is that "at the name of Jesus every knee should bow,... and every tongue confess that Jesus Christ is Lord" (*Ph* 2:10-11); "to this end Christ died and lived again, that he might be Lord both of the dead and of the living"; "we shall all stand before the judgement seat of God" (*Rm* 14:9-11). Likewise Johannine teaching stresses that "The Father judges no one, but has given all judgement to the Son, that all may honour the Son, even as they honour the Father" (*Jn* 5:22-23); "I heard every creature in heaven and on earth and under the earth and in the sea, and all therein, saying: 'To him who sits upon

---

[118] The Fathers of the Church delight in reflecting on the assumption by Christ of the whole of humanity; e.g. Irenaeus, *Adv.Haer.* 3,19,3 (SCh 211, 380), *Epideixis* 33 (SCh 406, 130-131); Hilary of Poitiers, *In Mt.* 4,8 (SCh 254, 130); 18,6 (SCh 258, 80); *Trin.* II,24 (CCL 62, 60); *Tr.Ps.* 51,17; 54,9 (CCL 61, 104; 146); etc.; Gregory of Nyssa, *In Cant.* Or.II (Opera, ed. JAEGER, VI, 61); *Adv. Apoll.* (Opera III/1, 152); Cyril of Alexandria, *In Joh.Evang.* I,9 (PG 73, 161-164); Leo the Great, *Tract.* 64,3; 72,2 (CCL 138A, 392; 442f.).

[119] The Fathers had a salvific understanding of the Incarnation itself; e.g. Cyril of Alexandria, *Comm. in Joh.* 5 (PG 73, 753).

[120] See below, footnote 127.

the throne and to the Lamb be blessing and honour and glory and might for ever and ever!'" (*Rv* 5:13).

90. The Scriptures relate all humanity without exception to Christ. A major weakness of the traditional view of Limbo is that it is unclear whether the souls there have any relationship to Christ; the Christocentricity of the doctrine seems deficient. In some accounts, the souls in Limbo seem to have a natural happiness that belongs to a different order from the supernatural order in which people choose for or against Christ. This appears to be a feature of Aquinas' account, though Suarez and the later scholastics emphasised that Christ restores human nature (his grace is *gratia sanans*, healing of human nature) and thereby enables the very natural happiness that Aquinas attributed to the souls in Limbo. The grace of Christ was therefore implicit in Aquinas' account, though not developed. The later scholastics thereby envisaged three possible destinies (at least in practice, though in principle they might have accepted only two destinies: heaven and hell), and understood, against Augustine, that it was by the grace of Christ that the numerous infants in Limbo were there and not in hell!

91. Where sin abounded, grace superabounded! That is the emphatic teaching of Scripture, but the idea of Limbo seems to constrain that superabundance. "[T]he free gift is not like the trespass. For if many died through one man's trespass, much more have the grace of God and the free gift in the grace of that one man Jesus Christ abounded for many"; "as one man's trespass led to condemnation for all men, so one man's act of righteousness leads to acquittal and life for all men"; "where sin increased, grace abounded all the more" (*Rm* 5:15, 18, 20). "For as in Adam all die, so also in Christ shall all be made alive" (1 *Co* 15:22). Scripture teaches of our sinful solidarity in Adam, yes, but it does so as the backdrop to teaching our salvific solidarity in Christ. 'The doctrine of original sin is, so to speak, the "reverse side" of the Good News that Jesus is the saviour of all men, that all need salvation and that salvation is offered to all through Christ.'[121] Many traditional accounts of sin and salvation (and of Limbo) have stressed solidarity with Adam more than solidarity with Christ or at least such accounts have

[121] *CCC* 389.

had a restrictive conception of the ways by which human beings benefit from solidarity with Christ. This would seem to have been a characteristic of Augustine's thought in particular:[122] Christ saves a select few from the mass who are damned in Adam. The teaching of St Paul would urge us to redress the balance and to centre humanity on Christ the saviour, to whom all, in some way, are united.[123] "He who is the 'image of the invisible God'[124] is himself the perfect man who has restored in the children of Adam that likeness to God which had been disfigured ever since the first sin. Human nature, by the very fact that it was assumed, not absorbed, in him, has been raised in us also to a dignity beyond compare" (*GS* 22). We wish to stress that humanity's solidarity with Christ (or, more properly, Christ's solidarity with all of humanity) must have priority over the solidarity of human beings with Adam, and that the question of the destiny of unbaptised infants who die must be addressed in that light.

92. "He is the image of the invisible God, the first-born of all creation; for in him all things were created, in heaven and on earth, visible and invisible,... all things were created through him and for him. He is before all things, and in him all things hold together. He is the head of the body, the Church; he is the beginning, the first-born from the dead, that in everything he might be pre-eminent" (*Col* 1:15-18). God's plan is "to unite all things in him, things in heaven and things on earth" (*Ep* 1:10). There is a renewed appreciation of the great cosmic mystery of communion in Christ. This, in fact, is the fundamental context for our question.

93. Nevertheless, human beings are blessed with freedom, and a free acceptance of Christ is the ordinary means of salvation; we are not saved without our acceptance and certainly not against our will. All adults either explicitly or implicitly make a decision *vis-à-vis* Christ who has united himself with them (cf. *GS* 22). Some modern

---

[122] E.g. Augustine, *Enarr. In Ps.70*, II, 1 (PL 36, 891): *"omnis autem homo Adam; sicut in his qui crediderunt, omnis homo Christus, quia membra sunt Christi"*. This text shows Augustine's difficulty in regarding solidarity with Christ as universally as solidarity with Adam. All have solidarity with Adam; those who believe have solidarity with Christ. Irenaeus is more even-handed in his doctrine of recapitulation; cf. *Adv.Haer.* 3, 21, 10; 5, 12, 3; 5, 14, 2; 5, 15, 4; 5, 34, 2.

[123] By the fact of the Incarnation, cf. *GS* 22.

[124] Col 1:15; cf. 2 Co 4:4.

theologians see the option for or against Christ as implicated in all choices. However, it is precisely the lack of free-will and responsible choice on the part of infants that leads to the query as to how they stand *vis-à-vis* Christ if they die unbaptised. The fact that infants can enjoy the vision of God is recognised in the practice of baptizing infants. The traditional view is that it is only through sacramental Baptism that infants have solidarity with Christ and hence access to the vision of God. Otherwise, solidarity with Adam has priority. We may ask, however, how that view might be changed if priority were restored to our solidarity with Christ (i.e. Christ's solidarity with us).

94. Baptism for salvation can be received either *in re* or *in voto*. It is traditionally understood that the implicit choice for Christ that adults who are not actually baptised can make constitutes a *votum* for Baptism and is salvific. In the traditional view, such an option is not open to infants who have not attained the use of free-will. The supposed impossibility of Baptism *in voto* for infants is central to the whole question. Hence, many, many attempts have been made in modern times to explore the possibility of a *votum* in the case of an unbaptised infant, either a *votum* exercised on behalf of the infant by its parents or by the Church,[125] or perhaps a *votum* exercised by the infant in some way.[126] The Church has never ruled out such a solution, and attempts to get Vatican II to do so significantly failed, because of a widespread sense that investigation of this matter was still ongoing and a widespread desire to entrust such infants to the mercy of God.

95. It is important to recognise a "double gratuity" which calls us into being and simultaneously calls us to eternal life. Though a purely natural order is conceivable, no human life is actually lived in such an order. The actual order is supernatural; channels of

---

[125] See below, 3.4.

[126] With regard to the possibility of a *votum* on the part of the infant, growth towards free-will might perhaps be imagined as a continuum which unfolds towards maturity from the first moment of existence, rather than there being a sudden qualitative jump to the exercise of mature, responsible decision. The existence of the unborn is a continuum of human life and growth; it does not suddenly become human at some point. Consequently, infants may actually be capable of exercising some kind of rudimentary *votum* by analogy with that of unbaptised adults. Some theologians have understood the mother's smile to mediate the love of God to the infant, and have therefore seen the infant's response to that smile as a response to God himself. Some modern psychologists and neurologists are convinced that the infant in the womb is already in some way conscious and has some use of freedom. Cf. V. FRANKL, *Der unbewusste Gott. Psychotherapie und Religion,* München 1979; D. AMEN, *Healing the Hardware of the Soul,* New York 2002.

grace are open from the very beginning of each human life. All are born with that humanity which was assumed by Christ himself and all live in some kind of relation to him, with different degrees of explicitness (cf. *LG* 16) and acceptance, at every moment. There are two possible ends for a human being in such an order: either the vision of God or hell (cf. *GS* 22). Though some medieval theologians maintained the possibility of an intermediate, natural, destiny, gained by the grace of Christ (*gratia sanans*), namely Limbo,[127] we consider such a solution problematic and wish to indicate that other approaches are possible, based on hope for a redemptive grace given to unbaptised infants who die which opens for them the way to heaven. We believe that, in the development of doctrine, the solution in terms of Limbo can be surpassed in view of a greater theological hope.

3.4. The Church and the Communion of Saints

96. Because all people live in some kind of relation to Christ (cf. *GS* 22), and the Church is the body of Christ, all people live also in some kind of relation to the Church at every moment. The Church has a profound solidarity or communion with the whole of humanity (cf. *GS* 1). She lives with a dynamic orientation to the fulness of life with God in Christ (cf. *LG* chap.7), and wills to draw all people into that fulness of life. The Church is, in fact, 'the universal sacrament of salvation' (*LG* 48, cf. 1, 9). Salvation is social (cf. *GS* 12), and the Church already lives the graced life of the communion of saints to which all are called, and embraces all people in all circumstances in her prayer, most especially when she celebrates the Eucharist. The Church includes in her prayer non-Christian adults and non-baptised infants who die. Very significantly, the pre-Vatican II lack of liturgical prayers for unbaptised infants who die, has been remedied since the Council.[128] Bound in a common *sensus fidei* (cf. *LG* 12), the Church reaches out to all, knowing them to be loved by God. An important reason for the failure of attempts to get Vatican II to teach that unbaptised infants are definitely deprived of the vision of God[129] was the testimony of bishops that that was not the faith of their people; it did not correspond to the *sensus fidelium*.

---

[127] See above, para 90.

[128] See below, 3.5.

[129] See above, Chapter 1.6.

97. St Paul teaches that the unbelieving husband or wife of a Christian believer is "consecrated" through their wife or husband, respectively, and moreover that their children too are "holy" (1 *Co* 7:14). This is a remarkable indication that the holiness that resides in the Church reaches out to people outside the visible bounds of the Church by means of the bonds of human communion, in this case the family bonds between husband and wife in marriage and parents and children. St Paul implies that the spouse and the child of a believing Christian have by that very fact at least a connection to membership of the Church and to salvation; their family situation "involves a certain introduction to the Covenant".[130] His words give no assurance of salvation for the unbaptised spouse (cf. 1 *Co* 7:16) or child, but surely, once again, grounds for hope.

98. When an infant is baptised, he or she cannot personally make a profession of faith. Rather, at that moment, the parents and the Church as a whole provide a context of faith for the sacramental action. Indeed, St Augustine teaches that it is the Church that presents a child for baptism.[131] The Church professes her faith and intercedes powerfully for the infant, supplying the act of faith that the infant is unable to make; again the bonds of communion, both natural and supernatural, are operative and manifest. If an unbaptised infant is incapable of a *votum baptismi*, then by the same bonds of communion the Church might be able to intercede for the infant and express a *votum baptismi* on his or her behalf that is effective before God. Moreover, the Church effectively does express in her liturgy just such a *votum* by the very charity towards all that is renewed in her in every celebration of the Eucharist.

99. Jesus taught: "unless one is born of water and the Spirit, he cannot enter the kingdom of God" (*Jn* 3:5); from which we understand the need for sacramental Baptism.[132] Likewise, he said: "unless you eat the flesh of the Son of man and drink his blood, you have no life in you" (*Jn* 6:53); from which we understand the (closely related) need for participation in the Eucharist. However, just as we do not conclude from the latter words that someone who

---

[130] Y. Congar, *Vaste monde ma paroisse*, 171.

[131] Cf. Augustine, *First Letter to Boniface*, 22, 40 (PL 44, 570).

[132] Cf. footnote 94 above.

has not received the sacrament of the Eucharist cannot be saved, so we should not deduce from the former words that someone who has not received the sacrament of Baptism cannot be saved. What we should conclude is that no-one is saved without some relation to Baptism and Eucharist, and therefore to the Church which is defined by these sacraments. All salvation has some relation to Baptism, Eucharist and the Church. The principle that there is "no salvation outside the Church" means that there is no salvation which is not from Christ and ecclesial by its very nature. Likewise, the scriptural teaching that "without faith it is impossible to please [God]" (*Heb* 11:6) indicates the intrinsic role of the Church, the communion of faith, in the work of salvation. It is especially in the liturgy of the Church that this role becomes manifest, as the Church prays and intercedes for all, including unbaptised infants who die.

3.5. *Lex Orandi, Lex Credendi*

100. Before Vatican II, in the Latin Church, there was no Christian funeral rite for unbaptised infants and such infants were buried in unconsecrated ground. Strictly speaking, there was no funeral rite for baptised infants either, but in their case a Mass of the Angels was celebrated and of course they were given a Christian burial. Thanks to the liturgical reform after the Council, the *Roman Missal* now has a funeral Mass for a child who died before Baptism, and there are also special prayers for such a situation in the *Ordo Exsequiarum*. Though the tone of the prayers in both instances is noticeably cautious, it is now the case that the Church liturgically expresses hope in the mercy of God, to whose loving care the infant is entrusted. This liturgical prayer both reflects and shapes the *sensus fidei* of the Latin Church regarding the fate of unbaptised infants who die: *lex orandi, lex credendi*. Significantly, in the Greek Catholic Church there is only one funeral rite for infants whether baptised or not yet baptised, and the Church prays for all deceased infants that they may be received into the bosom of Abraham where there is no sorrow or anguish but only eternal life.

101. "As regards children who have died without Baptism, the Church can only entrust them to the mercy of God, as she does in her funeral rites for them. Indeed, the great mercy of God who desires that all should be saved, and Jesus' tenderness toward children

which caused him to say: 'Let the children come to me, do not hinder them' (*Mk* 10:14; cf.1 *Tm* 2:4), allow us to hope that there is a way of salvation for children who have died without Baptism. All the more urgent is the Church's call not to prevent little children coming to Christ through the gift of holy Baptism".[133]

3.6. Hope

102. Within the hope that the Church bears for the whole of humanity and wants to proclaim afresh to the world of today, is there a hope for the salvation of infants who die without Baptism? We have carefully re-considered this complex question, with gratitude and respect for the responses that have been given through the history of the Church, but also with an awareness that it falls to us to give a coherent response for today. Reflecting within the one tradition of faith that unites the Church through the ages, and relying utterly on the guidance of the Holy Spirit whom Jesus promised would lead his followers "into all the truth" (*Jn* 16:13), we have sought to read the signs of the times and to interpret them in the light of the Gospel. Our conclusion is that the many factors that we have considered above give serious theological and liturgical grounds for hope that unbaptised infants who die will be saved and enjoy the Beatific Vision. We emphasise that these are reasons for prayerful *hope*, rather than grounds for sure knowledge. There is much that simply has not been revealed to us (cf. *Jn* 16:12). We live by faith and hope in the God of mercy and love who has been revealed to us in Christ, and the Spirit moves us to pray in constant thankfulness and joy (cf. 1 *Th* 5:18).

103. What has been revealed to us is that the ordinary way of salvation is by the sacrament of Baptism. None of the above considerations should be taken as qualifying the necessity of Baptism or justifying delay in administering the sacrament.[134] Rather, as we want to reaffirm in conclusion, they provide strong grounds for hope that God will save infants when we have not been able to do for them what we would have wished to do, namely, to baptize them into the faith and life of the Church.

---

[133] *CCC* 1261.

[134] Cf. *CCC* 1257.

CTS Church Documents Service

The easiest way to keep up to date with the teaching of the Church. Fast and economical to your door.

How does it work?

- There is no joining fee, your details are simply added to our list of subscribers to the service.
- You will then receive all the major Vatican and Bishops' Conference of England and Wales documents with invoice (payable within 30 days).
- There is no minimum term of membership.
- Simply complete the form below to receive each new title as soon as it is published.

I would like to Subscribe to the CTS Church Documents Service

Name: ....

Address: ....

....

Post Code:...............................

Tel:............................ Email: ....